March of America Facsimile Series

No. 13

The Journey of Coronado

Pedro Castañeda

The Journey of Coronado
by Pedro Castañeda

ANN ARBOR
UNIVERSITY MICROFILMS, INC.
A Subsidiary of Xerox Corporation

Foreword

The Journey of Coronado 1540-1542 concerns the expedition led by the Spanish explorer Francisco Vázquez Coronado to locate the reportedly fabulously wealthy Indian cities in what is now the southwestern United States. Coronado dispelled illusions about the great store of precious metals held by the Indians of the region, but he also opened up a vast new area of the North American continent to public knowledge and greatly extended Spanish penetration northward.

Friar Marcos, a missionary who claimed to have come within sight of one of the seven cities of Cibola, had returned to Mexico City with dazzling accounts of the great wealth possessed by this and by the other Indian cities. Mendoza, the viceroy in Mexico, ordered Coronado to lead an expedition to find them. Coronado departed northward in 1540 with several thousand men in his company. The expedition fought battle after battle with the Indians as it proceeded, although Coronado reported that, in accordance with his orders, he treated the Indians as well as possible. When the Spaniards reached Chichilticalli, the view was anything but encouraging. Coronado found that the fame of the town "was summed up in one tumble down house without a roof." The village of Cibola was hardly more impressive. In anger and disappointment Coronado complained that Friar Marcos had "not told the truth in a single thing that he said, but everything is the reverse." The soldiers, infuriated with the Friar, compelled him to leave the expedition.

In spite of Coronado's misgivings about the prospect of acquiring gold and silver, an Indian guide restored the spirits of many with glowing tales of the wealth of Quivira. But when Coronado arrived in that country, located in what is now the state of Kansas, he found it to contain nothing more of value than he had seen in any of the previous Indian towns. After arranging to have the untruthful Indian guide garroted, Coronado began the long homeward march. The Viceroy received Coronado coolly and according to one report Coronado's "reputation was gone from this time on."

Pedro Castañeda, a soldier of the expedition, has furnished the principal account of Coronado's explorations. A 16th-century copy of the original manuscript, on which this modern English translation is based, is among the holdings of the New York Public Library. The present edition also contains numerous letters of Coronado to his superiors describing the progress of the expedition, and other contemporaneous correspondence and reports about it. A map showing the route taken by Coronado and a historical introduction by the translator, George Parker Winship, accompany the texts. Winship has supplied additional detail in his article "The Coronado Expedition, 1540-1542," in the *Fourteenth Annual Report of the Bureau of Ethnology to the Secretary of the Smithsonian Institution* (Washington, 1896), Part I, pp. 329-613. See also George P. Hammond's edition of the *Narratives of the Coronado Expedition* (Albuquerque, 1940).

The Journey of Coronado

LES SINGVLARITEZ

Toreau
sauuage.

tre cefte Floride & la riuiere de Palme fe trouuent
diuerfes efpeces de beftes monftrueufes: entre lefquel-
les lon peut voir vne efpece de grands taureaux, por-

tans cornes longues feulement d'vn pié, & fur le dos
vne tumueur ou eminence, come vn chameau: le poil
long par tout le corps, duquel la couleur s'approche fort
de celle d'vne mule fauue. & encores l'eft plus celuy
qui eft deffoubs le mentō. Lon en amena vne fois deux
tous vifs en Efpagne, de l'vn defquels j'ay d eu la peau
& non autre chofe, & n'y peurent viure long temps.
Ceft animal ainfi que lon dit, eft perpetuel ennemy du
cheual, & ne le peut endurer pres de luy. De la Floride tirant au promontoire de Baxe, fe trouue quelque
petite riuiere, ou les efclaues vont pefcher huitres, qui
portent perles. Or depuis que fommes venus iufque là,
que de toucher la collection des huitres, ne veux ou-
blier par quel moyen, les parles en font tirées, tant au
index

Cap de
Baxe.

Huitres
portans
perles.

THE BUFFALO

(From Thevet's "Les Singularitez de la France Antarctique,"
Antwerp, 1558. Winsor considers this one of the earliest, if
not the earliest, picture of the buffalo.)

The

Journey of Coronado
1540-1542

from the City of Mexico to the
Grand Canon of the Colorado
and the Buffalo Plains of Texas,
Kansas and Nebraska

As told by himself and his followers

TRANSLATED AND EDITED
WITH AN INTRODUCTION
BY
George Parker Winship

WITH MAP

MCMXXII
ALLERTON BOOK CO.
New York

INTRODUCTION

THE narratives printed in the present volume tell the story of one of the most remarkable explorations recorded in the annals of American history. Seventy-five years before the English succeeded in establishing themselves on the northeastern coast of North America, a band of Spaniards, starting from what was already a populous and flourishing colony at the City of Mexico, penetrated the opposite extreme of the continent, and explored thoroughly a region as extensive as the coast line of the United States from Maine to Georgia.

The accounts of their experiences printed herewith were all written by members of the expedition. With two exceptions they were written during the journey, and were the official reports prepared by the general and sent to the viceroy in Mexico or the emperor-king in Spain, or by the lieutenants in charge of special explorations. The first and principal narrative was written for the purpose of providing a history of the expedition, by one of the common soldiers some time after his return to Mexico, when he apparently felt that there was danger that posterity would forget the deeds of those with whom

he had toiled and suffered in the vain search
for something which would reward their
costly undertaking. All that is known of
the author, Pedro Castañeda, beyond what
he relates in this narrative, is that he was a
native of the Biscayan town of Najera in
northern Spain, who had established himself
in the Spanish outpost at Culiacan, in northwestern Mexico, at the time Coronado organ-
ized his expedition, and that he was the
father of eight surviving children, who, with
their mother, presented in 1554 a claim
against the Mexican treasury, on account of
the father's exploits. The Spanish text of
Castañeda's history is preserved in the Lenox
Library, now absorbed into the New York
Public Library. It is printed, together with
the translations reprinted herewith, in the
Fourteenth Annual Report of the United
States Bureau of Ethnology, Washington,
D. C., 1896, a volume which has long been
out of print. In the present book many
passages in these translations have been re-
vised and corrected. The editor is under
obligations to Mr. F. W. Hodge of the
Smithsonian Institution, Mr. W. M. Tipton
of Santa Fé, Mr. Charles F. Lummis of Los
Angeles, and Mr. Ripley Hitchcock and Mr.
F. S. Dellenbaugh of New York, for sugges-
tions and assistance in regard to these im-
provements in the text.

In February, 1540, the army whose for-
tunes are recounted in these narratives assembled at Compostela, on the Pacific coast
west of Mexico city. When it passed in

review before the viceroy Mendoza, who had
provided the funds and equipment, the general in command, Francisco Vazquez Coronado, rode at the head of some two hundred
and fifty horsemen and seventy Spanish foot
soldiers armed with crossbows and harquebuses. Besides these there were three hundred or more native allies, and upward of a
thousand negro and Indian servants and followers, to lead the spare horses, drive the
pack mules, carry the extra luggage, and
herd the droves of oxen and cows, sheep and
swine.

The expedition started on February 23d,
and a month later, on Easter day, it entered
Culiacan, then the northwestern out-post
of European civilization, half way up the
mainland coast of the Gulf of California.
Here Coronado reorganized his force and,
toward the end of April, he started northward into the unknown country with a
picked force of two hundred men equipped
for rapid marching, leaving the rest to follow
at the slower pace of the pack trains and the
four-footed food supplies. Following the
river courses up stream, the advance party
was soon deep in the mountains. For two
long months they persistently pushed ahead,
the inhospitable country steadily growing
worse. Eventually other streams showed
them the way out on to a level district
crossed by well-worn trails which led them
toward the "Seven Cities of Cibola." These
were the goal of whose fame they had heard
from the Franciscan friar, Marcos of Nice,

who had viewed them from a distant hill-
top two years previously, and who now accompanied the expedition as guide and chap-
lain.

It was perhaps on July 4th, 1540, that
Coronado drew up his force in front of the
first of the "Seven Cities," and after a sharp
fight forced his way into the stronghold, the
stone and adobe-built pueblo of Hawikuh,
whose ruins can still be traced on a low hillock a few miles southwest of the village
now occupied by the New Mexican Zuñi
Indians. Here the Europeans camped for
several weeks, seeking rest, refreshment, and
news of the land. A small party was sent
off toward the northwest, where another
group of seven villages was found in the
region still occupied by the descendants of
the people whom the Spaniards visited, the
Moqui tribes of Tusayan. As a result of
the information secured here, another party
journeyed westward until its progress was
stopped by the Grand Cañon of the Colorado,
then seen for the first time by Europeans.
Explorations were also made toward the east,
where the river villages along the Rio Grande
were found to be larger and better stocked
with food supplies than the settlements at
Cibola-Zuñi. Coronado therefore moved his
headquarters to the largest of these river
towns, Tiguex, near the modern Bernalillo, a
short distance north of Albuquerque. Here,
as the winter of 1540–41 was setting in, he
was rejoined by the main body of the army,
which had laboriously followed the trail of

its general through the mountains and across the desert.

In one of the river villages Coronado found an Indian slave who said he was a native of Quivira, which he described as a rich and populous place far away in the east. Acting upon this information, with the Indian as a guide, Coronado started on April 23d, 1541, with his whole army to march to Quivira. From Cicuye or Pecos, whose ruins can still be seen by the traveller from the Atchison, Topeka and Santa Fé trains, the guide seems to have led the white men down the Pecos River until they were out of the mountains, and on to the vast plains where they soon met the countless herds of bison or "humpbacked oxen." For five weeks the Europeans plodded onward across what is now known as the "Staked Plains," following a generally easterly direction.

They had probably crossed the upper branches of the Colorado River of Texas and reached the head waters of the Nueces, when Coronado became convinced that his guide was endeavoring to lose him in this limitless expanse of rolling prairie. The food supplies were beginning to run low, and so the army was ordered to return to the villages on the Rio Grande. Some of the natives of the plains, met with on the march, had answered the questions about Quivira by pointing toward the north. That no chance might be left untried, the general selected thirty of the freshest and best-mounted of his men to

accompany him in a search in that direction.
For forty-two days they followed the compass
needle, whose variation probably took them
about three degrees west of a true northward
course. At last their guides told them that
they had reached Quivira, when they were
not far from Great Bend on the Arkansas
River, whose course they had followed from
the neighborhood of Dodge City. It was a
village of Wichita Indian tepees.

Coronado spent a month in exploring the
surrounding country, moving his camp to a
larger village further north, and sending out
messengers and reconnoitering parties in all
directions. Having assured himself that
there was nothing to reward his search, he
returned to the main body of his army, the
Quiviran guides leading him by a much
shorter route, along the line of the famous
Santa Fé trail, to the Rio Grande. Every
clew which promised anything of value to
the Spaniards had been followed to its ut-
most, without revealing anything which
they desired. In the spring of 1542 Coronado started back with his men to Cibola-
Zuñi, through the rough mountain passages
to the Gulf of California, and so on down to
the city of Mexico, where he arrived in the
early autumn, "very sad and very weary,
completely worn out and shame-faced." He
had failed to find any of the things for which
he went in search. But he had added to the
world as known to Europeans an extent of
country bounded on the west by the Colorado
River from its mouth to the Grand Cañon,

on the east by the boundless prairies, and
stretching northward to the upper waters of
the Rio Grande and the southern boundary
of Nebraska.

GEORGE PARKER WINSHIP.

SPANISH EXPLORATIONS.

*(For the use of this outline map and also the frontispiece
the publishers are indebted to the courtesy of Messrs. Ginn
& Co., publishers of "The Louisiana Purchase and the
Early History, Exploration and Building of the West," by
Ripley Hitchcock.)*

CONTENTS

CONTENTS

CONTENTS

CONTENTS

THIRD PART

CONTENTS

CONTENTS

CONTENTS

ITINERARY OF THE CORONADO EXPEDITIONS, 1527-1547

1527

JUNE 17   Narvaez sails from Spain to explore the mainland north of the Gulf of Mexico.

1528

APRIL 15   Narvaez lands in Florida.
SEPT. 22   The failure of the Narvaez expedition is assured.

1535

Cortes makes a settlement in Lower California.
Mendoza comes to Mexico as viceroy of New Spain.

1536

APRIL   Cabeza de Vaca and three other survivors of the Narvaez expedition arrive in New Spain.
The Licenciate de la Torre takes the residencia of Nuño de Guzman, who is imprisoned until June 30, 1538.

1537

Franciscan friars labor among the Indian tribes living north of New Spain.
Coronado subdues the revolted miners of Amatepeque.
The proposed expedition under Dorantes comes to naught.
APRIL 20   De Soto receives a grant of the mainland of Florida.

1538

SEPT.   It is rumored that Coronado has been
             nominated governor of New Galicia.

1539

             Pedro de Alvarado returns from Spain
             to the New World.
MARCH 7   Friar Marcos de Niza, accompanied by
             the negro Estevan, starts from Culia-
             can to find the Seven Cities.
APRIL 18   The appointment of Coronado as gov-
             ernor of New Galicia is confirmed.
MAY   De Soto sails from Habana.
MAY 9   Friar Marcos enters the wilderness of
             Arizona.
MAY 21   Friar Marcos learns of the death of
             Estevan.
MAY 25   De Soto lands on the coast of Florida.
JULY 8   Ulloa sails from Acapulco nearly to the
             head of the Gulf of California in com-
             mand of a fleet furnished by Cortes.
AUGUST   Friar Marcos returns from the north and
SEPT. 2   certifies to the truth of his report be-
             fore Mendoza and Coronado.
OCTOBER   The news of Niza's discoveries spreads
             through New Spain.
Nov.   Mendoza begins to prepare for an expe-
             dition to conquer the Seven Cities of
             Cibola.
             Melchior Diaz is sent to verify the re-
             ports of Friar Marcos.
             De Soto finds the remains of the camp
             of Narvaez at Bahia de los Cavallos.
Nov. 12   Witnesses in Habana describe the effect
             of the friar's reports.

1540

JAN. 1   Mendoza celebrates the new year at
             Pasquaro.
JAN. 9   Coronado at Guadalajara.
FEB. 5   Cortes stops at Habana on his way to
             Spain.
FEB.   The members of the Cibola expedition

	assemble at Compostela, where the viceroy finds them on his arrival.
FEB. 22.	Review of the army on Sunday.
FEB. 23.	The army, under the command of Francisco Vazquez Coronado, starts for Cibola (not on February 1).
FEB. 26.	Mendoza returns to Compostela, having left the army two days before, and examines witnesses to discover how many citizens of New Spain have accompanied Coronado. He writes a letter to King Charles V, which has been lost.
MARCH	The army is delayed by the cattle in crossing the rivers.
	The death of the army master, Samaniego, at Chiametla.
	Return of Melchior Diaz and Juan de Saldivar from Chichilticalli.
MARCH 3	Beginning of litigation in Spain over the right to explore and conquer the Cibola country.
MARCH 28	Reception to the army at Culiacan, on Easter day.
APRIL	The army is entertained by the citizens of Culiacan.
	Mendoza receives the report of Melchior Diaz' exploration, perhaps at Jacona.
	Coronado writes to Mendoza, giving an account of what has already happened, and of the arrangements which he has made for the rest of the journey. This letter has been lost.
APRIL 17	Mendoza writes to the Emperor Charles V.
APRIL 22	Coronado departs from Culiacan with about seventy-five horsemen and a few footmen.
APRIL MAY	Coronado passes through Petatlan, Cinaloa, Los Cedros, Yaquemi, and other places mentioned by Jaramillo.
MAY 9	Alarcon sails from Acapulco to coöperate with Coronado. The army starts from Culiacan and marches toward the Corazones or Hearts valley.
MAY 26	Coronado leaves the valley of Corazones.
JUNE	He proceeds to Chichilticalli, passing

Senora or Sonora and Ispa, and thence crosses the Arizona wilderness, fording many rivers.

The army builds the town of San Hieronimo in Corazones valley.

JULY 7   Coronado reaches Cibola and captures the first city, the pueblo of Hawikuh, which he calls Granada.

JULY 11   The Indians retire to their stronghold on Thunder mountain.

JULY 15   Pedro de Tovar goes to Tusayan or Moki, returning within thirty days.

JULY 19   Coronado goes to Thunder mountain and returns the same day.

AUG. 3   Coronado writes to Mendoza. He sends Juan Gallego to Mexico, and Melchior Diaz to Corazones with orders for the army. Friar Marcos accompanies them.

AUG. 25 (?) Lopez de Cardenas starts to find the canyons of Colorado river, and is gone about eighty days.

AUG. 26   Alarcon enters the mouth of Colorado river.

AUG. 29   Hernando de Alvarado goes eastward to Tiguex, on the Rio Grande, and to the buffalo plains.

Pedro de Alvarado arrives in New Spain.

SEPT. 7   Hernando de Alvarado reaches Tiguex.

Diaz and Gallego reach Corazones about the middle of September, and the army starts for Cibola.

Coronado visits Tutahaco.

SEPT. TO   The army reaches Cibola, and goes
JANUARY   thence to Tiguex for its winter quarters. The natives in the Rio Grande pueblos revolt and are subjugated. The Turk tells the Spaniards about Quivira.

OCTOBER   Diaz starts from Corazones before the end of September, with twenty five men, and explores the country along the Gulf of California, going beyond Colorado river.

Diego de Alcaraz is left in command of the town of San Hieronimo.

Nov. 29   Mendoza and Pedro de Alvarado sign an agreement in regard to common exploration and conquests.

1541

JAN. 8   Diaz dies on the return from the mouth of the Colorado, and his companions return to Corazones valley.

MARCH   Alcaraz, during the spring, moves the village of San Hieronimo from Corazones valley to the valley of Suya river.

APRIL 20   Beginning of the Mixton war in New Galicia.

Coronado writes a letter to the King from Tiguex, which has been lost.

Tovar and perhaps Gallego return to Mexico.

APRIL 23   Coronado starts with all his force from Tiguex to cross the buffalo plains to Quivira.

MAY   The army is divided somewhere on the great plains, perhaps on Canadian river. The main body returns to Tiguex, arriving there by the middle or last of June.

De Soto crosses the Mississippi.

JUNE   Coronado, with thirty horsemen, rides north to Quivira, where he arrives forty-two (?) days later.

JUNE 24   Pedro de Alvarado is killed at Nochistlan, in New Galicia.

AUGUST   Coronado spends about twenty-five days in the country of Quivira, leaving "the middle or last of August."

SEPT 28   The Indians in New Galicia attack the town of Guadalajara, but are repulsed.

OCT. 2   Coronado returns from Quivira to Tiguex and writes a letter to the King.

Nov.   Cardenas starts to return to Mexico with some other invalids from the army. He finds the village of Suya in ruins and hastily returns to Tiguex.

DECEMBER   Coronado falls from his horse and is seriously injured.

The Mixton peñol is surrendered by the revolted Indians during holiday week.

1542

Coronado and his soldiers determine to return to New Spain. They start in the spring, and reach Mexico probably late in the autumn. The general makes his report to the viceroy, who receives him coldly. Coronado not long after resigns his position as governor of New Galicia and retires to his estates.

APRIL 17 De Soto reaches the mouth of Red river, where he dies, May 21.

JUNE 27 Cabrillo starts on his voyage up the California coast. He dies in January, 1543, and the vessels return to New Spain by April, 1544.

NOV. 1 Villalobos starts across the Pacific. His fleet meets with many misfortunes and losses. The survivors, five years or more later, return to Spain.

NOV. 25 Friar Juan de la Cruz is killed at Tiguex, where he remained when the army departed for New Spain. Friar Luis also remained in the new country, at Cicuye, and Friar Juan de Padilla, at Quivira, where he is killed.

The companions of Friar Juan de Padilla make their way back to Mexico, arriving before 1552.

1544

NOV. 30 Promulgation of the New Laws for the Indies.

Sebastian Cabot publishes his map of the New World.

1547

Mendoza, before he leaves New Spain to become viceroy of Peru, answers the charges preferred against him by the officials appointed to investigate his administration.

TRANSLATION OF THE NARRATIVE OF CASTAÑEDA

Account of the expedition to Cibola which took place in the year 1540, in which all those settlements, their ceremonies and customes, are described. Written by Pedro de Castañeda, of Najera.

PREFACE

To me it seems very certain, my very noble lord, that it is a worthy ambition for great men to desire to know and wish to preserve for posterity correct information concerning the things that have happened in distant parts, about which little is known. I do not blame those inquisitive persons who, perchance with good intentions, have many times troubled me not a little with their requests that I clear up for them some doubts which they have had about different things that have been commonly related concerning the events and occurrences that took place during the expedition to Cibola, or the New Land, which the good viceroy—may he be with God in His glory [1]—Don Antonio de Mendoza, ordered and arranged, and on which he sent Francisco Vazquez de Coronado as captain-general.

In truth, they have reason for wishing to know the truth, because most people very often make things of which they have heard, and about which they have perchance no knowledge, appear either greater or less than they are. They make nothing of those

[1] Mendoza died in Lima, July 21, 1552.

things that amount to something, and those
that do not they make so remarkable that
they appear to be something impossible to
believe. This may very well have been
caused by the fact that, as that country was
not permanently occupied, there has not been
anyone who was willing to spend his time in
writing about its peculiarities, because all
knowledge was lost of that which it was not
the pleasure of God—He alone knows the
reason—that they should enjoy.

In truth, he who wishes to employ himself thus in writing out the things that happened on the expedition, and the things that
were seen in those lands, and the ceremonies
and customs of the natives, will have matter
enough to test his judgment, and I believe
that the result can not fail to be an account
which, describing only the truth, will be so
remarkable that it will seem incredible.

And besides, I think that the twenty
years and more since that expedition took
place have been the cause of some stories
which are related. For example, some make
it an uninhabitable country, others have it
bordering on Florida, and still others on
Greater India, which does not appear to be
a slight difference. They are unable to give
any basis upon which to found their statements. There are those who tell about
some very peculiar animals, who are contra-
dicted by others who were on the expedition, declaring that there was nothing of
the sort seen. Others differ as to the limits

of the provinces and even in regard to the
ceremonies and customs, attributing what
pertains to one people to others. All this
has had a large part, my very noble lord,
in making me wish to give now, although
somewhat late, a short general account for
all those who pride themselves on this noble
curiosity, and to save myself the time taken
up by these solicitations. Things enough
will certainly be found here which are hard
to believe. All or the most of these were
seen with my own eyes, and the rest is from
reliable information obtained by inquiry of
the natives themselves.

Understanding as I do that this little
work would be nothing in itself, lacking authority, unless it were favored and protected
by a person whose authority would protect
it from the boldness of those who, without
reverence, give their murmuring tongues
liberty, and knowing as I do how great are
the obligations under which I have always
been, and am, to your grace, I humbly beg
to submit this little work to your protection.
May it be received as from a faithful retainer
and servant.

It will be divided into three parts, that
it may be better understood. The first will
tell of the discovery and the armament or
army that was made ready, and of the whole
journey, with the captains who were there;
the second, of the villages and provinces
which were found, and their limits, and
ceremonies and customs, the animals, fruits,

THE ROUTE OF

CORONADO
- - - - - - - -

SCALE OF MILES.

0   50   100   200   300   400

Longitude   West   113°   from   Greenwich   109°   105°

and vegetation, and in what parts of the country these are; the third, of the return of the army and the reasons for abandoning the country, although these were insufficient, because this is the best place there is for discoveries—the marrow of the land in these western parts, as will be seen. And after this has been made plain, some remarkable things which were seen will be described at the end, and the way by which one might more easily return to discover that better land which we did not see, since it would be no small advantage to enter the country through the land which the Marquis of the Valley, Don Fernando Cortes, went in search of under the Western star, and which cost him no small sea armament.

May it please our Lord to so favor me that with my slight knowledge and small abilities I may be able by relating the truth to make my little work pleasing to the learned and wise readers, when it has been accepted by your grace. For my intention is not to gain the fame of a good composer or rhetorician, but I desire to give a faithful account and to do this slight service to your grace, who will, I hope, receive it as from a faithful servant and soldier, who took part in it. Although not in a polished style, I write that which happened—that which I heard, experienced, saw, and did.

I always notice, and it is a fact, that for the most part when we have something valuable in our hands, and deal with it

without hindrance, we do not value or prize
it as highly as if we understood how much
we would miss it after we had lost it, and
the longer we continue to have it the less
we value it; but after we have lost it and
miss the advantages of it, we have a great
pain in the heart, and we are all the time
imagining and trying to find ways and
means by which to get it back again. It
seems to me that this has happened to all
or most of those who went on the expedition
which, in the year of our Savior Jesus
Christ 1540, Francisco Vazquez Coronado
led in search of the Seven Cities.

Granted that they did not find the riches
of which they had been told, they found a
place in which to search for them and the
beginning of a good country to settle in, so
as to go on farther from there. Since they
came back from the country which they conquered and abandoned, time has given them
a chance to understand the direction and
locality in which they were, and the borders
of the good country they had in their hands,
and their hearts weep for having lost so favorable an opportunity. Just as men see
more at the bull fight when they are upon
the seats than when they are around in the
ring, now when they know and understand
the direction and situation in which they
were, and see, indeed, that they can not enjoy it nor recover it, now when it is too late
they enjoy telling about what they saw, and
even of what they realize that they lost,

especially those who are now as poor as
when they went there. They have never
ceased their labors and have spent their time
to no advantage. I say this because I have
known several of those who came back from
there who amuse themselves now by talking
of how it would be to go back and proceed
to recover that which is lost, while others
enjoy trying to find the reason why it was
discovered at all. And now I will proceed
to relate all that happened from the beginning.

THE JOURNEY OF CORONADO

FIRST PART

CHAPTER I

Treats of the way we first came to know about the Seven Cities, and of how Nuño de Guzman made an expedition to discover them.

In the year 1530 Nuño de Guzman, who was President of New Spain,[1] had in his possession an Indian, a native of the valley or valleys of Oxitipar, who was called Tejo by the Spaniards. This Indian said he was the son of a trader who was dead, but that when he was a little boy his father had gone into the back country with fine feathers to trade for ornaments, and that when he came back he brought a large amount of gold and silver, of which there is a good deal in that country. He went with him once or twice, and saw some very large villages, which he compared to Mexico and its environs. He had seen seven very large towns which had streets of silver workers. It took forty days to go

[1] President, or head, of the Audiencia, the administrative and judicial board which governed the province.

1

there from his country, through a wilderness
in which nothing grew, except some very
small plants about a span high. The way
they went was up through the country between the two seas, following the northern
direction. Acting on this information, Nuño
de Guzman got together nearly 400 Spaniards and 20,000 friendly Indians of New
Spain, and, as he happened to be in Mexico,
he crossed Tarasca, which is in the province
of Michoacan, so as to get into the region
which the Indian said was to be crossed
toward the North sea, in this way getting to
the country which they were looking for,
which was already named "The Seven Cities."
He thought, from the forty days of which
the Tejo had spoken, that it would be found
to be about 200 leagues, and that they would
easily be able to cross the country.

Omitting several things that occurred on
this journey, as soon as they had reached
the province of Culiacan, where his government ended and where the New Kingdom of
Galicia is now, they tried to cross the country, but found the difficulties very great, because the mountain chains which are near
that sea are so rough that it was impossible,
after great labor, to find a passageway in that
region. His whole army had to stay in the
district of Culiacan for so long on this account that some rich men who were with
him, who had possessions in Mexico, changed
their minds, and every day became more
anxious to return. Besides this, Nuño de

Guzman received word that the Marquis of the Valley, Don Fernando Cortes, had come from Spain with his new title,[1] and with great favors and estates, and as Nuño de Guzman had been a great rival of his at the time he was president,[2] and had done much damage to his property and to that of his friends, he feared that Don Fernando Cortes would want to pay him back in the same way, or worse. So he decided to establish the town of Culiacan there and to go back with the other men, without doing anything more.

After his return from this expedition, he founded Xalisco, where the city of Compostela is situated, and Tonala, which is called Guadalaxara,[3] and now this is the New Kingdom of Galicia. The guide they had, who was called Tejo, died about this time, and thus the name of these Seven Cities and the search for them remains until now, since they have not been discovered.[4]

[1] Marqués del Valle de Oaxaca y Capitan General de la Nueva España y de la Costa del Sur.

[2] Guzman had presided over the trial of Cortes, who was in Spain at the time, for the murder of his first wife seven years previously (October, 1522). See Zaragoza's edition of Suarez de Peralta's Tratado, p. 315.

[3] The name was changed in 1540.

[4] The best discussion of the stories of the Seven Caves and the Seven Cities is in Bandelier's Contributions, p. 9, ff.

CHAPTER II

Of how Francisco Vazquez Coronado came to be governor, and the second account which Cabeza de Vaca gave.

EIGHT years after Nuño de Guzman made this expedition, he was put in prison by a juez de residencia,[1] named the licentiate Diego de la Torre, who came from Spain with sufficient powers to do this.[2] After the death of the judge, who had also managed the government of that country himself, the good Don Antonio de Mendoza, viceroy of New Spain, appointed as governor of that province Francisco Vazquez de Coronado, a gentleman from Salamanca, who had married a lady in the city of Mexico, the daughter of Alonso de Estrada, the treasurer and at one time governor of Mexico, and the son, most people said, of His Catholic Majesty Don Ferdinand, and many stated it as certain. As I was saying, at the time Francisco Vazquez was appointed governor, he was traveling through New Spain as an official inspector, and in this way he gained the friendship of many worthy men who afterward went on his expedition with him.

[1] A judge appointed to investigate the accounts and administration of a royal official.
[2] A full account of the licentiate de la Torre and his administration is given by Mota Padilla (ed. Icazbalceta, pp. 103–106). He was appointed juez March 17, 1536, and died during 1538.

4

It happened that just at this time three Spaniards, named Cabeza de Vaca, Dorantes, and Castillo Maldonado, and a negro, who had been lost on the expedition which Pamfilo de Narvaez led into Florida, reached Mexico.[1] They came out through Culiacan, having crossed the country from sea to sea, as anyone who wishes may find out for himself by an account which this same Cabeza de Vaca wrote and dedicated to Prince Don Philip, who is now King of Spain and our sovereign.[2] They gave the good Don Antonio de Mendoza an extended account of some powerful villages, four and five stories high, of which they had heard a great deal in the countries they had crossed, and other things very different from what turned out to be the truth. The noble viceroy communicated this to the new governor, who gave up the visits he had in hand, on account of this, and hurried his departure for his government, taking with him the negro who had come [with Cabeza de Vaca] with the three friars of the order of Saint Francis, one of whom was named Friar Marcos of Nice, a regular priest, and another Friar Daniel, a lay brother, and the other Friar Antonio de Santa Maria. When he reached the province of Culiacan he sent the friars just men-

[1] They appeared in New Spain in April, 1536, before Coronado's appointment. Castañeda may be right in the rest of his statement.
[2] This account has been translated by Buckingham Smith, New York, 1871.

tioned and the negro, who was named Stephen, off in search of that country, because Friar Marcos offered to go and see it, because he had been in Peru at the time Don Pedro de Alvarado went there overland.

It seems that, after the friars I have mentioned and the negro had started, the negro did not get on well with the friars, because he took the women that were given him and collected turquoises, and got together a stock of everything. Besides, the Indians in those places through which they went got along with the negro better, because they had seen him before. This was the reason he was sent on ahead to open up the way and pacify the Indians, so that when the others came along they had nothing to do except to keep an account of the things for which they were looking.

CHAPTER III

Of how they killed the negro Stephen at Cibola, and Friar Marcos returned in flight.

AFTER Stephen had left the friars, he thought he could get all the reputation and honor himself, and that if he should discover those settlements with such famous high houses, alone, he would be considered bold and courageous. So he proceeded with the people who had followed him, and attempted to cross the wilderness which lies between the country he had passed through and Cibola. He was so far ahead of the friars that, when these reached Chichilticalli, which is on the edge of the wilderness, he was already at Cibola, which is 80 leagues beyond. It is 220 leagues from Culiacan to the edge of the wilderness, and 80 across the desert, which makes 300, or perhaps 10 more or less. As I said, Stephen reached Cibola loaded with the large quantity of turquoises they had given him and some beautiful women whom the Indians who followed him and carried his things were taking with them and had given him. These had followed him from all the settlements he had passed, believing that under his protection they could traverse the whole world without any danger.

But as the people in this country were more intelligent than those who followed Stephen, they lodged him in a little hut they had outside their village, and the older men and the governors heard his story and took steps to find out the reason he had come to that country. For three days they made inquiries about him and held a council. The account which the negro gave them of two white men who were following him, sent by a great lord, who knew about the things in the sky, and how these were coming to instruct them in divine matters, made them think that he must be a spy or a guide from some nations who wished to come and conquer them, because it seemed to them unreasonable to say that the people were

7

white in the country from which he came and that he was sent by them, he being black. Besides these other reasons, they thought it was hard of him to ask them for turquoises and women, and so they decided to kill him. They did this, but they did not kill any of those who went with him, although they kept some young fellows and let the others, about 60 persons, return freely to their own country. As these, who were badly scared, were returning in flight, they happened to come upon the friars in the desert 60 leagues from Cibola, and told them the sad news, which frightened them so much that they would not even trust these folks who had been with the negro, but opened the packs they were carrying and gave away everything they had except the holy vestments for saying mass. They returned from here by double marches, prepared for anything, without seeing any more of the country except what the Indians told them.

CHAPTER IV

Of how the noble Don Antonio de Mendoza made an expedition to discover Cibola.

AFTER Francisco Vazquez Coronado had sent Friar Marcos of Nice and his party on the search already related, he was engaged in Culiacan about some business that related to his government, when he heard an account of a province called Topira,[1] which was to the north of the country of Culiacan. He started to explore this region with several of the conquerors and some friendly Indians, but he did not get very far, because the mountain chains which they had to cross were very difficult. He returned without finding the least signs of a good country, and when he got back, he found the friars who had just arrived, and who told such great things about what the negro Stephen had discovered and what they had heard from the Indians, and other things they had heard about the South sea and islands and other riches, that, without stopping for anything, the governor set off at once for the City of Mexico, taking Friar Marcos with him, to tell the viceroy about it. He made the things seem more important by not talking about them to anyone except his particular friends, under promise of the greatest secrecy, until after he had reached Mexico and seen Don Antonio de Mendoza. Then it began to be noised abroad that the Seven Cities for which Nuño de Guzman had searched, had already been discovered, and a beginning was made in collecting an armed force and in bringing together people to go to conquer them.

The noble viceroy arranged with the friars of the order of Saint Francis so that

[1] Bandelier (Contributions, p. 104) says this was Topia, in Durango, a locality since noted for its rich mines.

Friar Marcos was made father provincial, as a result of which the pulpits of that order were filled with such accounts of marvels and wonders that more than 300 Spaniards and about 800 natives of New Spain collected in a few days. There were so many men of such high quality among the Spaniards, that such a noble body was never collected in the Indies, nor so many men of quality in such a small body, there being 300 men. Francisco Vazquez Coronado, governor of New Galicia, was captain-general, because he had been the author of it all. The good viceroy Don Antonio did this because at this time Francisco Vazquez was his closest and most intimate friend, and because he considered him to be wise, skillful, and intelligent, besides being a gentleman. Had he paid more attention and regard to the position in which he was placed and the charge over which he was placed, and less to the estates he left behind in New Spain, or, at least, more to the honor he had and might secure from having such gentlemen under his command, things would not have turned out as they did. When this narrative is ended, it will be seen that he did not know how to keep his position nor the government that he held.

CHAPTER V

Concerning the captains who went to Cibola.

WHEN the viceroy, Don Antonio de Mendoza, saw what a noble company had come together, and the spirit and good will with which they had all presented themselves, knowing the worth of these men, he would have liked very well to make every one of them captain of an army; but as the whole number was small he could not do as he would have liked, and so he issued the commissions and captaincies as he saw fit, because it seemed to him that if they were appointed by him, as he was so well obeyed and beloved, nobody would find fault with his arrangements. After everybody had heard who the general was, he made Don Pedro de Tovar ensign general, a young gentleman who was the son of Don Fernando de Tovar, the guardian and lord high steward of the Queen Doña Juana, our demented mistress—may she be in glory—and Lope de Samaniego, the governor of the arsenal at Mexico,[1] a gentleman fully equal to the charge, army-master. The captains were Don Tristan de Arellano; Don Pedro de Guevara, the son of Don Juan de Guevara and nephew of the Count of Oñate; Don

[1] See Mendoza's letter to the King, regarding Samaniego's position.

Garcia Lopez de Cardenas; Don Rodrigo
Maldonado, brother-in-law of the Duke of
the Infantado; Diego Lopez, alderman of
Seville, and Diego Gutierres, for the
cavalry.

All the other gentlemen were placed under the flag of the general, as being distinguished persons, and some of them became
captains later, and their appointments were
confirmed by order of the viceroy and by the
general, Francisco Vazquez. To name some
of them whom I happen to remember, there
were Francisco de Barrionuevo, a gentleman
from Granada; Juan de Saldivar, Francisco
de Ovando, Juan Gallego, and Melchior Diaz
—a captain who had been mayor of Culiacan,
who, although he was not a gentleman,
merited the position he held. The other
gentlemen, who were prominent, were Don
Alonso Manrique de Lara; Don Lope de Urrea, a gentleman from Aragon; Gomez Suarez
de Figueroa, Luis Ramirez de Vargas, Juan
de Sotomayor, Francisco Gorbalan, the com-
missioner Riberos, and other gentlemen, men
of high quality, whom I do not now recall.
The infantry captain was Pablo de Melgosa
of Burgos, and of the artillery, Hernando de
Alvarado of the mountain district. As I
say, since then I have forgotten the names
of many gentlemen. It would be well if I
could name some of them, so that it might
be clearly seen what cause I had for saying
that they had on this expedition the most
brilliant company ever collected in the In-

dies to go in search of new lands. But they were unfortunate in having a captain who left in New Spain estates and a pretty wife, a noble and excellent lady, which were not the least causes for what was to happen.

CHAPTER VI

Of how all the companies collected in Compostela and set off on the journey in good order.

WHEN the viceroy Don Antonio de Mendoza had fixed and arranged everything as we have related, and the companies and captaincies had been arranged, he advanced a part of their salaries from the chest of His Majesty to those in the army who were in greatest need. And as it seemed to him that it would be rather hard for the friendly Indians in the country if the army should start from Mexico, he ordered them to assemble at the city of Compostela, the chief city in the New Kingdom of Galicia, 110 leagues from Mexico, so that they could begin their journey there with everything in good order. There is nothing to tell about what happened on this trip, since they all finally assembled at Compostela by shrove-tide, in the year (fifteen hundred and) forty-one.[1]

---

[1] The correct date is 1540. Castañeda carries the error throughout the narrative.

After the whole force had left Mexico, he ordered Don Pedro de Alarcon to set sail with two ships that were in the port of La Natividad on the South seacoast, and go to the port of Xalisco to take the baggage which the soldiers were unable to carry,[1] and thence to sail along the coast near the army, because he had understood from the reports that they would have to go through the country near the seacoast, and that we could find the harbors by means of the rivers, and that the ships could always get news of the army, which turned out afterward to be false, and so all this stuff was lost, or, rather, those who owned it lost it, as will be told farther on. After the viceroy had completed all his arrangements, he set off for Compostela, accompanied by many noble and rich men. He kept the New Year of (fifteen hundred and) forty-one at Pasquaro, which is the chief place in the bishopric of Michoacan, and from there he crossed the whole of New Spain, taking much pleasure in enjoying the festivals and great receptions which were given him, till he reached Compostela, which is, as I have said, 110 leagues. There he found the whole company assembled, being well treated and entertained by Christobal de Oñate, who had the whole charge of that government for the time being. He had had the management of it and was in command of all that

[1] See the instructions given by Mendoza to Alarcon, in Buckingham Smith's Florida, p. 1.

region when Francisco Vazquez was made governor.[1]

All were very glad when he arrived, and he made an examination of the company.and found all those whom we have mentioned. He assigned the captains to their companies, and after this was done, on the next day, after they had all heard mass, captains and soldiers together, the viceroy made them a very eloquent short speech, telling them of the fidelity they owed to their general and showing them clearly the benefits which this expedition might afford, from the conversion of those peoples as well as in the profit of those who should conquer the territory, and the advantage to His Majesty and the claim which they would thus have on his favor and aid at all times. After he had finished, they all, both captains and soldiers, gave him their oaths upon the Gospels in a Missal that they would follow their general on this expedition and would obey him in everything he commanded them, which they faithfully performed, as will be seen. The next day after this was done, the army started off with its colors flying. The viceroy, Don Antonio, went with them for two days, and there he took leave of them, returning to New Spain with his friends.

[1] See the writings of Tello and Mota Padilla concerning Oñate. Much of the early prosperity of New Galicia—what there was of it—seems to have been due to Oñate's skillful management.

CHAPTER VII

Of how the army reached Chiametla, and the killing of the army-master, and the other things that happened up to the arrival at Culiacan.

AFTER the viceroy Don Antonio left them, the army continued its march. As each one was obliged to transport his own baggage and all did not know how to fasten the packs, and as the horses started off fat and plump, they had a good deal of difficulty and labor during the first few days, and many left many valuable things, giving them to anyone who wanted them, in order to get rid of carrying them. In the end necessity, which is all powerful, made them skillful, so that one could see many gentlemen become carriers, and anybody who despised this work was not considered a man.

With such labors, which they then thought severe, the army reached Chiametla, where it was obliged to delay several days to procure food. During this time the army-master, Lope de Samaniego, went off with some soldiers to find food, and at one village, a crossbowman having entered it indiscreetly in pursuit of the enemies, they shot him through the eye and it passed through his brain, so that he died on the spot. They also shot five or six of his companions before Diego Lopez, the alderman from Seville, since the commander was dead, collected the men and sent word to the general. He put a guard in the village and over the provisions. There was great confusion in the army when this news became known. He was buried here. Several sorties were made, by which food was obtained and several of the natives taken prisoners. They hanged those who seemed to belong to the district where the army-master was killed.

It seems that when the general, Francisco Vazquez, left Culiacan with Friar Marcos to tell the viceroy, Don Antonio de Mendoza, the news, as already related, he left orders for Captain Melchior Diaz and Juan de Saldivar to start off with a dozen good men from Culiacan and verify what Friar Marcos had seen and heard. They started and went as far as Chichilticalli, which is where the wilderness begins, 220 leagues from Culiacan, and there they turned back, not finding anything important. They reached Chiametla just as the army was ready to leave, and reported to the general. Although they were kept secret, the bad news leaked out, and there were some reports which, although they were exaggerated, did not fail to give an indication of what the facts were.[1] Friar Marcos, noticing that some were feel-

[1] The report of Diaz is incorporated in the letter from Mendoza to the King, translated herein. This letter seems to imply that Diaz stayed at Chichilticalli; but if such was his intention when writing the report to Mendoza, he must have changed his mind and returned with Saldivar as far as Chiametla.

ing disturbed, cleared away these clouds, promising that what they would see should be good, and that he would place the army in a country where their hands would be filled, and in this way he quieted them so that they appeared well satisfied. From there the army marched to Culiacan, making some detours into the country to seize provisions. They were two leagues from the town of Culiacan at Easter vespers, when the inhabitants came out to welcome their governor and begged him not to enter the town till the day after Easter.

CHAPTER VIII

Of how the army entered the town of Culiacan and the reception it received, and other things which happened before the departure.

WHEN the day after Easter came, the army started in the morning to go to the town and, as they approached, the inhabitants of the town came out on to an open plain with foot and horse drawn up in ranks as if for a battle, and having its seven bronze pieces of artillery in position, making a show of defending their town. Some of our soldiers were with them. Our army drew up in the same way and began a skirmish with them, and after the artillery on both sides had been fired they were driven back, just as if the town had been taken by force of arms, which was a pleasant demonstration of welcome,

18

except for the artilleryman who lost a hand by a shot, from having ordered them to fire before he had finished drawing out the ram-rod.

After the town was taken, the army was well lodged and entertained by the towns-people, who, as they were all very well-to-do people, took all the gentlemen and people of quality who were with the army into their own apartments, although they had lodgings prepared for them all just outside the town. Some of the townspeople were not ill repaid for this hospitality, because all had started with fine clothes and accoutrements, and as they had to carry provisions on their animals after this, they were obliged to leave their fine stuff, so that many preferred giving it to their hosts instead of risking it on the sea by putting it in the ship that had fol-lowed the army along the coast to take the extra baggage, as I have said. After they arrived and were being entertained in the town, the general, by order of the viceroy Don Antonio, left Fernandarias de Saabedra, uncle of Hernandarias de Saabedra, count of Castellar, formerly mayor of Seville, as his lieutenant and captain in this town. The army rested here several days, because the inhabitants had gathered a good stock of provisions that year and each one shared his stock very gladly with his guests from our army. They not only had plenty to eat here, but they also had plenty to take away with them, so that when the departure came they started off with more than six hundred loaded animals, besides the friendly Indians and the servants—more than a thousand persons. After a fortnight had passed, the general started ahead with about fifty horsemen and a few foot soldiers and most of the Indian allies, leaving the army, which was to follow him a fortnight later, with Don Tristan de Arellano in command as his lieutenant.

At this time, before his departure, a pretty sort of thing happened to the general, which I will tell for what it is worth. A young soldier named Trugillo (Truxillo) pretended that he had seen a vision while he was bathing in the river. Feigning that he did not want to, he was brought before the general, whom he gave to understand that the devil had told him that if he would kill the general, he could marry his wife, Doña Beatris, and would receive great wealth and other very fine things. Friar Marcos of Nice preached several sermons on this, laying it all to the fact that the devil was jealous of the good which must result from this journey and so wished to break it up in this way. It did not end here, but the friars who were in the expedition wrote to their convents about it, and this was the reason the pulpits of Mexico proclaimed strange rumors about this affair.

The general ordered Truxillo to stay in that town and not to go on the expedition, which was what he was after when he made

up that falsehood, judging from what afterward appeared to be the truth. The general
started off with the force already described
to continue his journey, and the army followed him, as will be related.

CHAPTER IX

Of how the army started from Culiacan and the
arrival of the general at Cibola and of the army at
Señora and of other things that happened.

THE general, as has been said, started to
continue his journey from the valley of Culiacan somewhat lightly equipped, taking
with him the friars, since none of them
wished to stay behind with the army. After
they had gone three days, a regular friar who
could say mass, named Friar Antonio Vic-
toria, broke his leg, and they brought him
back from the camp to have it doctored. He
stayed with the army after this, which was
no slight consolation for all. The general
and his force crossed the country without
trouble, as they found everything peaceful,
because the Indians knew Friar Marcos and
some of the others who had been with Melchior Diaz when he went with Juan de Saldibar to investigate.

After the general had crossed the inhabited region and came to Chichilticalli, where
the wilderness begins, and saw nothing favorable, he could not help feeling somewhat
downhearted, for, although the reports were

very fine about what was ahead, there was nobody who had seen it except the Indians who went with the negro, and these had already been caught in some lies. Besides all this, he was much affected by seeing that the fame of Chichilticalli was summed up in one tumble-down house without any roof, although it appeared to have been a strong place at some former time when it was inhabited, and it was very plain that it had been built by a civilized and warlike race of strangers who had come from a distance. This building was made of red earth. From here they went on through the wilderness, and in fifteen days came to a river about 8 leagues from Cibola, which they called Red River,[1] because its waters were muddy and reddish. In this river they found mullets like those of Spain. The first Indians from that country were seen here—two of them, who ran away to give the news. During the night following the next day, about 2 leagues from the village, some Indians in a safe place yelled so that, although the men were ready for anything, some were so excited that they put their saddles on hindside before; but these were the new fellows. When the veterans had mounted and ridden round the camp, the Indians fled. None of them could be caught because they knew the country.

[1] Bandelier, in his Gilded Man, identifies this with Zuñi river. The Rio Vermejo of Jaramillo is the Little Colorado or Colorado Chiquito.

The next day they entered the settled
country in good order, and when they saw
the first village, which was Cibola, such
were the curses that some hurled at Friar
Marcos that I pray God may protect him
from them.

It is a little, crowded village, looking as
if it had been crumpled all up together.
There are ranch houses in New Spain which
make a better appearance at a distance.[1] It
is a village of about 200 warriors, is three
and four stories high, with the houses small
and having only a few rooms, and without
a courtyard.   One yard serves for each section.   The people of the whole district had
collected here, for there are seven villages
in the province, and some of the others
are even larger and stronger than Cibola.
These folks waited for the army, drawn up
by divisions in front of the village.   When
they refused to have peace on the terms
the interpreters extended to them, but

[1] Mota Padilla, p. 113: "They reached Tzibola,
which was a village divided into two parts, which
were encircled in such a way as to make the village
round, and the houses adjoining three and four
stories high, with doors opening on a great court or
plaza, leaving one or two doors in the wall, so as to
go in and out.   In the middle of the plaza there is a
hatchway or trapdoor, by which they go down to a
subterranean hall, the roof of which was of large
pine beams, and a little hearth in the floor, and the
walls plastered.   The Indian men stayed there days
and nights playing (or gaming) and the women
brought them food; and this was the way the Indians of the neighboring villages lived."

appeared defiant, the Santiago [1] was given, and they were at once put to flight. The Spaniards then attacked the village, which was taken with not a little difficulty, since they held the narrow and crooked entrance. During the attack they knocked the general down with a large stone, and would have killed him but for Don Garcia Lopez de Cardenas and Hernando de Alvarado, who threw themselves above him and drew him away, receiving the blows of the stones, which were not few. But the first fury of the Spaniards could not be resisted, and in less than an hour they entered the village and captured it. They discovered food there, which was the thing they were most in need of. [2] After this the whole province was at peace.

The army which had stayed with Don Tristan de Arellano started to follow their general, all loaded with provisions, with lances on their shoulders, and all on foot, so as to have the horses loaded. With no slight labor from day to day, they reached a province which Cabeza de Vaca had named Hearts (Corazones), because the people here offered him many hearts of animals. He founded a town here and named it San

[1] The war cry or "loud invocation addressed to Saint James before engaging in battle with the Infidels."—Captain John Stevens' Dictionary.

[2] Compare the translation of the Traslado de las Nuevas herein. There are some striking resemblances between that account and Castañeda's narrative.

Hieronimo de los Corazones (Saint Jerome
of the Hearts). After it had been started,
it was seen that it could not be kept up here,
and so it was afterward transferred to a valley which had been called Señora.[1] The
Spaniards call it Señora, and so it will be
known by this name.

From here a force went down the river to
the seacoast to find the harbor and to find
out about the ships. Don Rodrigo Maldonado, who was captain of those who went in
search of the ships, did not find them, but
he brought back with him an Indian so large
and tall that the best man in the army
reached only to his chest. It was said that
other Indians were even taller on that coast.
After the rains ceased the army went on to
where the town of Señora was afterward located, because there were provisions in that
region, so that they were able to wait there
for orders from the general.

About the middle of the month of October[2] Captains Melchior Diaz and Juan Gallego came from Cibola, Juan Gallego on his
way to New Spain and Melchior Diaz to
stay in the new town of Hearts, in command
of the men who remained there. He was to
go along the coast in search of the ships.

[1] The persistent use of the form Señora, Madame,
for the place Sonora, may be due to the copyists.
[2] This should be September.

25

CHAPTER X

Of how the army started from the town of Señora, leaving it inhabited, and how it reached Cibola, and of what happened to Captain Melchior Diaz on his expedition in search of the ships and how he discovered the Tison (Firebrand) river.

AFTER Melchior Diaz and Juan Gallego had arrived in the town of Señora, it was announced that the army was to depart for Cibola; that Melchior Diaz was to remain in charge of that town with 80 men; that Juan Gallego was going to New Spain with messages for the viceroy, and that Friar Marcos was going back with him, because he did not think it was safe for him to stay in Cibola, seeing that his report had turned out to be entirely false, because the kingdoms that he had told about had not been found, nor the populous cities, nor the wealth of gold, nor the precious stones which he had reported, nor the fine clothes, nor other things that had been proclaimed from the pulpits. When this had been announced, those who were to remain were selected and the rest loaded their provisions and set off in good order about the middle of September on the way to Cibola following their general.

Don Tristan de Arellano stayed in this new town with the weakest men, and from this time on there was nothing but mutinies and strife, because after the army had gone Captain Melchior Diaz took 25 of the most efficient men, leaving in his place one Diego de Alcaraz, a man unfitted to have people under his command. He took guides and went toward the north and west in search of the seacoast. After going about 150 leagues, they came to a province of exceedingly tall and strong men—like giants. They are naked and live in large straw cabins built underground like smoke houses, with only the straw roof above ground. They enter these at one end and come out at the other. More than a hundred persons, old and young, sleep in one cabin. When they carry anything, they can take a load of more than three or four hundredweight on their heads. Once when our men wished to fetch a log for the fire, and six men were unable to carry it, one of these Indians is reported to have come and raised it in his arms, put it on his head alone, and carried it very easily.[1] They eat bread cooked in the ashes, as big as the large two-pound loaves of Castile. On account of the great cold, they carry a firebrand (tison) in

[1] Fletcher, in The World Encompassed by Sir Francis Drake, p. 131 (ed. 1854) tells a similar story of some Indians whom Drake visited on the coast of California: " Yet are the men commonly so strong of body, that that which 2 or 3 of our men could hardly beare, one of them would take vpon his backe, and without grudging, carrie it easily away, vp hill and downe hill an English mile together." Mota Padilla, cap. xxxii., p. 158, describes an attempt to catch one of these Indians.

the hand when they go from one place to another, with which they warm the other hand and the body as well, and in this way they keep shifting it every now and then.[1] On this account the large river which is in that country was called Rio del Tison (Firebrand River). It is a very great river and is more than 2 leagues wide at its mouth; here it is half a league across. Here the captain heard that there had been ships at a point three days down toward the sea. When he reached the place where the ships had been, which was more than 15 leagues up the river from the mouth of the harbor, they found written on a tree: "Alarcon reached this place; there are letters at the foot of this tree." He dug up the letters and learned from them how long Alarcon had waited for news of the army and that he had gone back with the ships to New Spain, because he was unable to proceed farther, since this sea was a bay, which was formed by the Isle of the Marquis,[2] which is called California, and it was explained that California was not an island, but a point of the mainland forming the other side of that gulf.

After he had seen this, the captain turned back to go up the river, without going down to the sea to find a ford by which to cross

[1] Father Sedelmair, in his Relacion, mentions this custom of the Indians. (See Bandelier, Final Report, vol. i., p. 108.)
[2] Cortes.

28

to the other side, so as to follow the other
bank. After they had gone five or six days,
it seemed to them as if they could cross on
rafts. For this purpose they called together
a large number of the natives, who were
waiting for a favorable opportunity to make
an attack on our men, and when they saw
that the strangers wanted to cross, they
helped make the rafts with all zeal and diligence, so as to catch them in this way on
the water and drown them or else so divide
them that they could not help one another.
While the rafts were being made, a soldier
who had been out around the camp saw a
large number of armed men go across to a
mountain, where they were waiting till the
soldiers should cross the river. He reported
this, and an Indian was quietly shut up, in
order to find out the truth, and when they
tortured him he told all the arrangements
that had been made. These were, that
when our men were crossing and part of
them had got over and part were on the
river and part were waiting to cross, those
who were on the rafts should drown those
they were taking across and the rest of their
force should make an attack on both sides of
the river. If they had had as much discre-
tion and courage as they had strength and
power, the attempt would have succeeded.

When he knew their plan, the captain had
the Indian who had confessed the affair killed
secretly, and that night he was thrown into
the river with a weight, so that the Indians

would not suspect that they were found out.
The next day they noticed that our men suspected them, and so they made an attack,
shooting showers of arrows, but when the
horses began to catch up with them and the
lances wounded them without mercy and
the musketeers likewise made good shots,
they had to leave the plain and take to the
mountain, until not a man of them was to
be seen. The force then came back and
crossed all right, the Indian allies and the
Spaniards going across on the rafts and the
horses swimming alongside the rafts, where
we will leave them to continue their journey.

To relate how the army that was on its
way to Cibola got on: Everything went
along in good shape, since the general had
left everything peaceful, because he wished
the people in that region to be contented and
without fear and willing to do what they
were ordered. In a province called Vacapan
there was a large quantity of prickly pears,
of which the natives make a great deal of
preserves.[1] They gave this preserve away
freely, and as the men of the army ate much
of it, they all fell sick with a headache and
fever, so that the natives might have done
much harm to the force if they had wished.
This lasted regularly twenty-four hours.
After this they continued their march until

[1] The Zunis make a similar sort of preserves from
the fruit of the tuna and the yucca. See Cushing in
The Millstone, Indianapolis, July, 1884, pp. 108-109.

they reached Chichilticalli. The men in the advance guard saw a flock of sheep one day after leaving this place. I myself saw and followed them. They had extremely large bodies and long wool; their horns were very thick and large, and when they run they throw back their heads and put their horns on the ridge of their back. They are used to the rough country, so that we could not catch them and had to leave them.

Three days after we entered the wilderness we found a horn on the bank of a river that flows in the bottom of a very steep, deep gully, which the general had noticed and left there for his army to see, for it was six feet long and as thick at the base as a man's thigh. It seemed to be more like the horn of a goat than of any other animal. It was something worth seeing. The army proceeded and was about a day's march from Cibola when a very cold tornado came up in the afternoon, followed by a great fall of snow, which was a bad combination for the carriers. The army went on till it reached some caves in a rocky ridge, late in the evening. The Indian allies, who were from New Spain, and for the most part from warm countries, were in great danger. They felt the coldness of that day so much that it was hard work the next day taking care of them, for they suffered much pain and had to be carried on the horses, the soldiers walking. After this labor the army reached Cibola, where their general was waiting for them, with their quarters all ready, and here they were reunited, except some captains and men who had gone off to discover other provinces.

CHAPTER XI

How Don Pedro de Tovar discovered Tusayan or Tutahaco [1] and Don Garcia Lopez de Cardenas saw the Firebrand river and the other things that had happened.

WHILE the things already described were taking place, Cibola being at peace, the General Francisco Vazquez found out from the people of the province about the provinces that lay around it, and got them to tell their friends and neighbors that Christians had come into the country, whose only desire was to be their friends, and to find out about good lands to live in, and for them to come to see the strangers and talk with them. They did this, since they know how to communicate with one another in these regions, and they informed him about a province with seven villages of the same sort as theirs, although somewhat different. They had nothing to do with these people. This province is called Tusayan. It is twenty-five leagues from Cibola. The villages are high and the people are warlike.

The general had sent Don Pedro de Tovar

[1] Compare chapter 13. These two groups of pueblos were not the same.

to these villages with seventeen horsemen and three or four foot soldiers. Juan de Padilla, a Franciscan friar, who had been a fighting man in his youth, went with them. When they reached the region, they entered the country so quietly that nobody observed them, because there were no settlements or farms between one village and another and the people do not leave the villages except to go to their farms, especially at this time, when they had heard that Cibola had been captured by very fierce people, who travelled on animals which ate people. This information was generally believed by those who had never seen horses, although it was so strange as to cause much wonder. Our men arrived after nightfall and were able to conceal themselves under the edge of the village, where they heard the natives talking in their houses. But in the morning they were discovered and drew up in regular order, while the natives came out to meet them, with bows, and shields, and wooden clubs, drawn up in lines without any confusion. The interpreter was given a chance to speak to them and give them due warning, for they were very intelligent people, but nevertheless they drew lines and insisted that our men should not go across these lines toward their village.[1]

[1] Compare the lines which the Hopi or Moqui Indians still mark with sacred meal during their festivals, as described by Dr. Fewkes in his "Few Summer Ceremonials," in vol. ii. of the Journal of American Ethnology and Archæology.

While they were talking, some men acted as if they would cross the lines, and one of the natives lost control of himself and struck a horse a blow on the cheek of the bridle with his club. Friar Juan, fretted by the time that was being wasted in talking with them, said to the captain: "To tell the truth, I do not know why we came here." When the men heard this, they gave the Santiago so suddenly that they ran down many Indians and the others fled to the town in confusion. Some indeed did not have a chance to do this, so quickly did the people in the village come out with presents, asking for peace. The captain ordered his force to collect, and, as the natives did not do any more harm, he and those who were with him found a place to establish their headquarters near the village. They had dismounted here when the natives came peacefully, saying that they had come to give in the submission of the whole province and that they wanted him to be friends with them and to accept the presents which they gave him. This was some cotton cloth, although not much, because they do not make it in that district. They also gave him some dressed skins and corn meal, and pine nuts and corn and birds of the country. Afterward they presented some turquoises, but not many. The people of the whole district came together that day and submitted themselves, and they allowed him to enter their villages freely to visit, buy, sell, and barter with them.

It is governed like Cibola, by an assembly of the oldest men. They have their governors and generals. This was where they obtained the information about a large river, and that several days down the river there were some people with very large bodies.

As Don Pedro de Tovar was not commissioned to go farther, he returned from there and gave this information to the general, who dispatched Don Garcia Lopez de Cardenas with about twelve companions to go to see this river. He was well received when he reached Tusayan and was entertained by the natives, who gave him guides for his journey. They started from here loaded with provisions, for they had to go through a desert country before reaching the inhabited region, which the Indians said was more than twenty days' journey. After they had gone twenty days they came to the banks of the river. It seemed to be more than 3 or 4 leagues in an air line across to the other bank of the stream which flowed between them.

This country was elevated and full of low twisted pines, very cold, and lying open toward the north, so that, this being the warm season, no one could live there on account of the cold. They spent three days on this bank looking for a passage down to the river, which looked from above as if the water was 6 feet across, although the Indians said it was half a league wide. It was impossible to descend, for after these three days Captain Melgosa and one Juan Galeras and another companion, who were the three lightest and most agile men, made an attempt to go down at the least difficult place, and went down until those who were above were unable to keep sight of them. They returned about 4 o'clock in the afternoon, not having succeeded in reaching the bottom on account of the great difficulties which they found, because what seemed to be easy from above was not so, but instead very hard and diffi-cult. They said that they had been down about a third of the way and that the river seemed very large from the place which they reached, and that from what they saw they thought the Indians had given the width correctly. Those who stayed above had estimated that some huge rocks on the sides of the cliffs seemed to be about as tall as a man, but those who went down swore that when they reached these rocks they were bigger than the great tower of Seville. They did not go farther up the river, because they could not get water.

Before this they had had to go a league or two inland every day late in the evening in order to find water, and the guides said that if they should go four days farther it would not be possible to go on, because there was no water within three or four days, for when they travel across this region themselves they take with them women loaded with

water in gourds, and bury the gourds of
water along the way, to use when they return, and besides this, they travel in one
day over what it takes us two days to accomplish.

This was the Tison (Firebrand) river,
much nearer its source than where Melchior
Diaz and his company crossed it. These
were the same kind of Indians, judging from
what was afterward learned. They came
back from this point and the expedition did
not have any other result. On the way
they saw some water falling over a rock and
learned from the guides that some bunches
of crystals which were hanging there were
salt. They went and gathered a quantity of
this and brought it back to Cibola, dividing
it among those who were there. They gave
the general a written account of what they
had seen, because one Pedro de Sotomayor
had gone with Don Garcia Lopez as chroni-
cler for the army. The villages of that province remained peaceful, since they were never
visited again, nor was any attempt made to
find other peoples in that direction.

CHAPTER XII

Of how people came from Cicuye to Cibola to see
the Christians, and how Hernando de Alvarado went
to see the cows.

WHILE they were making these discoveries, some Indians came to Cibola from
a village which was 70 leagues east of

this province, called Cicuye. Among them
was a captain who was called Bigotes
(Whiskers) by our men, because he wore a
long mustache. He was a tall, well-built
young fellow, with a fine figure. He told
the general that they had come in response
to the notice which had been given, to offer
themselves as friends, and that if we wanted
to go through their country they would consider us as their friends. They brought a
present of tanned hides and shields and head-
pieces, which were very gladly received, and
the general gave them some glass dishes and
a number of pearls and little bells which
they prized highly, because these were things
they had never seen. They described some
cows which, from a picture that one of them
had painted on his skin, seemed to be cows,
although from the hides this did not seem
possible, because the hair was woolly and
snarled so that we could not tell what sort
of skins they had. The general ordered
Hernando de Alvarado to take 20 companions and go with them, and gave him a
commission for eighty days, after which he
should return to give an account of what he
had found.[1]

Captain Alvarado started on this journey
and in five days reached a village which was
on a rock called Acuco,[2] having a popu-

[1] The report of Alvarado is probably the official
account of what he accomplished.

[2] In regard to the famous rock fortress of Acoma
see Bandelier's Introduction, p. 14, and his Final

lation of about 200 men. These people were robbers, feared by the whole country round about. The village was very strong, because it was up on a rock out of reach, having steep sides in every direction, and so high that it was a very good musket that could throw a ball as high. There was only one entrance by a stairway built by hand, which began at the top of a slope which is around the foot of the rock. There was a broad stairway for about 200 steps, then a stretch of about 100 narrower steps, and at the top they had to go up about three times as high as a man by means of holes in the rock, in which they put the points of their feet, holding on at the same time by their hands. There was a wall of large and small stones at the top, which they could roll down without showing themselves, so that no army could possibly be strong enough to capture the village. On the top they had room to sow and store a large amount of corn, and cisterns to collect snow and water. These people came down to the plain ready to fight, and would not listen to any arguments. They drew lines on the ground and determined to prevent our men from crossing these, but when they saw that they would have to fight they offered to make peace be-

Report, vol. i., p. 133. The Spaniards called it by a name resembling that which they heard applied to it in Zuñi-Cibola. The true Zuñi name of Acoma, on the authority of Mr. F. W. Hodge, is Hákukia; that of the Acoma people, Hákukwe.

fore any harm had been done. They went through their forms of making peace, which is to touch the horses and take their sweat and rub themselves with it, and to make crosses with the fingers of the hands. But to make the most secure peace they put their hands across each other, and they keep this peace inviolably. They made a present of a large number of [turkey] cocks with very big wattles, much bread, tanned deerskins, pine [piñon] nuts, flour [corn meal], and corn.

From here they went to a province called Triguex,[1] three days distant. The people all came out peacefully, seeing that Whiskers was with them. These men are feared throughout all those provinces. Alvarado sent messengers back from here to advise the general to come and winter in this country. The general was not a little relieved to hear that the country was growing better. Five days from here he came to Cicuye,[2] a very strong village four stories high. The people came out from the village with signs of joy to welcome Hernando de Alvarado and their captain, and brought them into the town with drums and pipes something like flutes,

[1] An error for Tiguex, at or near the present Bernalillo. Simpson located this near the mouth of the river Puerco, southeast of Acoma, but I follow Bandelier, according to whom Alvarado pursued a northeasterly direction from Acoma. See his Introduction, p. 30, and Final Report, vol. i., p. 129.

[2] Pecos. Besides his Final Report, vol. i., p. 127, see Bandelier's Report on the Pecos Ruins.

of which they have a great many. They
made many presents of cloth and turquoises,
of which there are quantities in that region.
The Spaniards enjoyed themselves here for
several days and talked with an Indian slave,
a native of the country toward Florida, which
is the region Don Fernando de Soto discovered. This fellow said that there were large
settlements in the farther part of that country. Hernando de Alvarado took him to
guide them to the cows; but he told them
so many and such great things about the
wealth of gold and silver in his country that
they did not care about looking for cows,
but returned after they had seen some few,
to report the rich news to the general.
They called the Indian "Turk," because he
looked like one.

Meanwhile the general had sent Don Garcia Lopez de Cardenas to Tiguex with men
to get lodgings ready for the army, which
had arrived from Señora about this time,
before taking them there for the winter; and
when Hernando de Alvarado reached Tiguex,
on his way back from Cicuye, he found Don
Garcia Lopez de Cardenas there, and so there
was no need for him to go farther. As it
was necessary that the natives should give
the Spaniards lodging places, the people in
one village had to abandon it and go to
others belonging to their friends, and they
took with them nothing but themselves and
the clothes they had on. Information was
obtained here about many towns up toward

the north, and I believe that it would have been much better to follow this direction than that of the Turk, who was the cause of all the misfortunes which followed.

CHAPTER XIII

Of how the general went toward Tutahaco with a few men and left the army with Don Tristan, who took it to Tiguex.

EVERYTHING already related had happened when Don Tristan de Arellano reached Cibola from Señora. Soon after he arrived, the general, who had received notice of a province containing eight villages, took 30 of the men who were most fully rested and went to see it, going from there directly to Tiguex with the skilled guides who conducted him. He left orders for Don Tristan de Arellano to proceed to Tiguex by the direct road, after the men had rested twenty days. On this journey, between one day when they left the camping place and midday of the third day, when they saw some snow-covered mountains, toward which they went in search of water, neither the Spaniards nor the horses nor the servants drank anything. They were able to stand it because of the severe cold, although with great difficulty. In eight days they reached Tutahaco,[1] where they learned that there were

[1] Coronado probably reached the Rio Grande near the present Isleta. Jaramillo applies this name to

42

other towns down the river. These people
were peaceful. The villages are terraced,
like those at Tiguex, and of the same style.

The general went up the river from here,
visiting the whole province, until he reached
Tiguex, where he found Hernando de Alvarado and the Turk. He felt no slight joy at
such good news, because the Turk said that
in his country there was a river in the level
country which was 2 leagues wide, in which
there were fishes as big as horses, and large
numbers of very big canoes, with more
than 20 rowers on a side, and that they
carried sails, and that their lords sat on the
poop under awnings, and on the prow they
had a great golden eagle. He said also that
the lord of that country took his afternoon
nap under a great tree on which were hung
a great number of little gold bells, which put
him to sleep as they swung in the air. He
said also that everyone had their ordinary
dishes made of wrought plate, and the jugs
and bowls were of gold. He called gold
acochis. For the present he was believed,
on account of the ease with which he told
it and because they showed him metal ornaments and he recognized them and said they
were not gold, and he knew gold and silver
very well and did not care anything about
other metals.

Açoma, and perhaps he is more correct, if we ought
to read it Tutahaio, since the Tiguas (the inhabitants
of Isleta, Sandia, Taos, and Picuris pueblos) call
Acoma Tuthea-uáy, according to Bandelier, Gilded
Man, p. 211.

The general sent Hernando de Alvarado back to Cicuye to demand some gold bracelets which this Turk said they had taken from him at the time they captured him. Alvarado went, and was received as a friend at the village, and when he demanded the bracelets they said they knew nothing at all about them, saying the Turk was deceiving him and was lying. Captain Alvarado, seeing that there were no other means, got the Captain Whiskers and the governor to come to his tent, and when they had come he put them in chains. The villagers prepared to fight, and let fly their arrows, denouncing Hernando de Alvarado, and saying that he was a man who had no respect for peace and friendship. Hernando de Alvarado started back to Tiguex, where the general kept them prisoners more than six months. This began the want of confidence in the word of the Spaniards whenever there was talk of peace from this time on, as will be seen by what happened afterward.

CHAPTER XIV

Of how the army went from Cibola to Tiguex and what happened to them on the way, on account of the snow.

WE have already said that when the general started from Cibola, he left orders for Don Tristan de Arellano to start twenty days later. He did so as soon as he saw that the men were well rested and provided with food and eager to start off to find their general. He set off with his force toward Tiguex, and the first day they made their camp in the best, largest, and finest village of that (Cibola) province.[1] This is the only village that has houses with seven stories. In this village certain houses are used as fortresses; they are higher than the others and set up above them like towers, and there are embrasures and loopholes in them for defending the roofs of the different stories, because, like the other villages, they do not have streets, and the flat roofs are all of a height and are used in common. The roofs have to be reached first, and these upper houses are the means of defending them. It began to snow on us there, and the force took refuge under the wings of the village, which extend out like balconies, with wooden pillars beneath, because they generally use ladders to go up to those balconies, since they do not have any doors below.

The army continued its march from here after it stopped snowing, and as the season had already advanced into December, during the ten days that the army was delayed, it did not fail to snow during the evenings and nearly every night, so that they had to clear away a large amount of snow when they came to where they wanted to make a camp.

[1] This was Matsaki, at the northwestern base of Thunder mountain, about 18 miles from Hawikuh, where the advance force had encamped.

The road could not be seen, but the guides managed to find it, as they knew the country. There are junipers and pines all over the country, which they used in making large brushwood fires, the smoke and heat of which melted the snow from 2 to 4 yards all around the fire. It was a dry snow, so that although it fell on the baggage and covered it for half a man's height it did not hurt it. It fell all night long, covering the baggage and the soldiers and their beds, piling up in the air, so that if any one had suddenly come upon the army nothing would have been seen but mountains of snow. The horses stood half buried in it. It kept those who were underneath warm instead of cold. The army passed by the great rock of Acuco, and the natives, who were peaceful, entertained our men well, giving them provisions and birds, although there are not many people here, as I have said. Many of the gentlemen went up to the top to see it, and they had great difficulty in going up the steps in the rock, because they were not used to them, for the natives go up and down so easily that they carry loads and the women carry water, and they do not seem even to touch their hands, although our men had to pass their weapons up from one to another.

From here they went on to Tiguex, where they were well received and taken care of, and the great good news of the Turk gave no little joy and helped lighten their hard labors, although when the army arrived we found the whole country or province in revolt, for reasons which were not slight in themselves, as will be shown, and our men had also burnt a village the day before the army arrived, and returned to the camp.

CHAPTER XV

Of why Tiguex revolted, and how they were punished, without being to blame for it.

IT has been related how the general reached Tiguex, where he found Don Garcia Lopez de Cardenas and Hernando de Alvarado, and how he sent the latter back to Cicuye, where he took the Captain Whiskers and the governor of the village, who was an old man, prisoners. The people of Tiguex did not feel well about this seizure.

In addition to this, the general wished to obtain some clothing to divide among his soldiers, and for this purpose he summoned one of the chief Indians of Tiguex, with whom he had already had much intercourse and with whom he was on good terms, who was called Juan Aleman by our men, after a Juan gentleman who lived in Mexico, whom he was said to resemble. The general told him that he must furnish about three hundred or more pieces of cloth, which he needed to give his people. He said that he was not able to do this, but that it pertained to the governors; and that besides this, they would have to consult together and divide it among the villages, and that it was necessary to make the demand of each town separately. The general did this, and ordered certain of the gentlemen who were with him to go and make the demand; and as there were twelve villages, some of them went on one side of the river and some on the other. As they were in very great need, they did not give the natives a chance to consult about it, but when they came to a village they demanded what they had to give, so that they could proceed at once. Thus these people could do nothing except take off their own cloaks and give them to make up the number demanded of them. And some of the soldiers who were in these parties, when the collectors gave them some blankets or cloaks which were not such as they wanted, if they saw any Indian with a better one on, they exchanged with him without more ado, not stopping to find out the rank of the man they were stripping, which caused not a little hard feeling.

Besides what I have just said, one whom I will not name, out of regard for him, left the village where the camp was and went to another village about a league distant, and seeing a pretty woman there he called her husband down to hold his horse by the bridle while he went up; and as the village was entered by the upper story, the Indian supposed he was going to some other part of it. While he was there the Indian heard

some slight noise, and then the Spaniard
came down, took his horse, and went away.
The Indian went up and learned that he had
violated, or tried to violate, his wife, and so
he came with the important men of the town
to complain that a man had violated his
wife, and he told how it happened. When
the general made all the soldiers and the
persons who were with him come together,
the Indian did not recognize the man, either
because he had changed his clothes or for
whatever other reason there may have been,
but he said that he could tell the horse, because he had held his bridle, and so he was
taken to the stables, and found the horse,
and said that the master of the horse must
be the man. He denied doing it, seeing
that he had not been recognized, and it may
be that the Indian was mistaken in the
horse; anyway, he went off without getting
any satisfaction.[1] The next day one of the
Indians, who was guarding the horses of the
army, came running in, saying that a companion of his had been killed, and that the
Indians of the country were driving off the
horses toward their villages. The Spaniards
tried to collect the horses again, but many
were lost, besides seven of the general's
mules.

The next day Don Garcia Lopez de Cardenas went to see the villages and talk with

---

[1] The instructions which Mendoza gave to Alarcon
show how carefully the viceroy tried to guard
against any such trouble with the natives.

the natives. He found the villages closed by palisades and a great noise inside, the horses being chased as in a bull fight and shot with arrows. They were all ready for fighting. Nothing could be done, because they would not come down on to the plain and the villages are so strong that the Spaniards could not dislodge them. The general then ordered Don Garcia Lopez de Cardenas to go and surround one village with all the rest of the force. This village was the one where the greatest injury had been done and where the affair with the Indian woman occurred. Several captains who had gone on in advance with the general, Juan de Saldivar and Barrionuevo and Diego Lopez and Melgosa, took the Indians so much by surprise that they gained the upper story, with great danger, for they wounded many of our men from within the houses. Our men were on top of the houses in great danger for a day and a night and part of the next day, and they made some good shots with their crossbows and muskets. The horsemen on the plain with many of the Indian allies from New Spain smoked them out from the cellars [1] into which they had broken, so that they begged for peace.

Pablo de Melgosa and Diego Lopez, the alderman from Seville, were left on the roof and answered the Indians with the same

[1] Evidently the underground, or partially underground, ceremonial chambers or kivas.

signs they were making for peace, which was to make a cross. They then put down their arms and received pardon. They were taken to the tent of Don Garcia, who, according to what he said, did not know about the peace and thought that they had given themselves up of their own accord because they had been conquered. As he had been ordered by the general not to take them alive, but to make an example of them so that the other natives would fear the Spaniards, he ordered 200 stakes to be prepared at once to burn them alive. Nobody told him about the peace that had been granted them, for the soldiers knew as little as he, and those who should have told him about it remained silent, not thinking that it was any of their business. Then when the enemies saw that the Spaniards were binding them and beginning to roast them, about a hundred men who were in the tent began to struggle and defend themselves with what there was there and with the stakes they could seize. Our men who were on foot attacked the tent on all sides, so that there was great confusion around it, and then the horsemen chased those who escaped. As the country was level, not a man of them remained alive, unless it was some who remained hidden in the village and escaped that night to spread throughout the country the news that the strangers did not respect the peace they had made, which afterward proved a great misfortune. After this was

over, it began to snow, and they abandoned
the village and returned to the camp just as
the army came from Cibola.

CHAPTER XVI

Of how they besieged Tiguex and took it and of
what happened during the siege.

As I have already related, it began to
snow in that country just after they captured
the village, and it snowed so much that for
the next two months it was impossible to do
anything except to go along the roads to advise them to make peace and tell them that
they would be pardoned and might consider
themselves safe, to which they replied that
they did not trust those who did not know
how to keep good faith after they had once
given it, and that the Spaniards should remember that they were keeping Whiskers
prisoner and that they did not keep their
word when they burned those who surrendered in the village.   Don Garcia Lopez de
Cardenas was one of those who went to give
this notice. He started out with about
30 companions and went to the village of
Tiguex to talk with Juan Aleman.   Although they were hostile, they talked with
him and said that if he wished to talk with
them he must dismount and they would
come out and talk with him about a peace,
and that if he would send away the horse-

men and make his men keep away, Juan
Aleman and another captain would come
out of the village and meet him. Everything was done as they required, and then
when they approached they said that they
had no arms and that he must take his off.
Don Garcia Lopez did this in order to give
them confidence, on account of his great desire to get them to make peace. When he
met them, Juan Aleman approached and
embraced him vigorously, while the other
two who had come with him drew two mal-
lets [1] which they had hidden behind their
backs and gave him two such blows over his
helmet that they almost knocked him sense-
less. Two of the soldiers on horseback had
been unwilling to go very far off, even when
he ordered them, and so they were near by
and rode up so quickly that they rescued
him from their hands, although they were
unable to catch the enemies because the
meeting was so near the village that of the
great shower of arrows which were shot at
them one arrow hit a horse and went
through his nose. The horsemen all rode
up together and hurriedly carried off their
captain, without being able to harm the
enemy, while many of our men were dan-
gerously wounded.

They then withdrew, leaving a number of
men to continue the attack. Don Garcia
Lopez de Cardenas went on with a part of

[1] Wooden warclubs shaped like potato-mashers.

the force to another village about half a league distant, because almost all the people in this region had collected into these two villages. As they paid no attention to the demands made on them except by shooting arrows from the upper stories with loud yells, and would not hear of peace, he returned to his companions whom he had left to keep up the attack of Tiguex. A large number of those in the village came out and our men rode off slowly, pretending to flee, so that they drew the enemy on to the plain, and then turned on them and caught several of their leaders. The rest collected on the roofs of the village and the captain returned to his camp.

After this affair the general ordered the army to go and surround the village. He set out with his men in good order, one day, with several scaling ladders. When he reached the village, he encamped his force near by, and then began the siege; but as the enemy had had several days to provide themselves with stores, they threw down such quantities of rocks upon our men that many of them were laid out, and they wounded nearly a hundred with arrows, several of whom afterward died on account of the bad treatment by an unskillful surgeon who was with the army. The siege lasted fifty days, during which time several assaults were made. The lack of water was what troubled the Indians most. They dug a very deep well inside the village, but were

not able to get water, and while they were
making it, it fell in and killed 30 persons.
Two hundred of the besieged died in the
fights. One day when there was a hard
fight, they killed Francisco de Obando, a
captain who had been army-master all the
time that Don Garcia Lopez de Cardenas was
away making the discoveries already described, and also Francisco Pobares, a fine
gentleman. Our men were unable to prevent them from carrying Francisco de Obando inside the village, which was regretted
not a little, because he was a distinguished
person, besides being honored on his own
account, affable and much beloved, which
was noticeable.

One day, before the capture was completed, they asked to speak to us, and said
that, since they knew we would not harm
the women and children, they wished to
surrender their women and sons, because
they were using up their water. It was impossible to persuade them to make peace,
as they said that the Spaniards would not
keep an agreement made with them. So
they gave up about a hundred persons, wom-
en and boys, who did not want to leave
them. Don Lope de Urrea rode up in front
of the town without his helmet and received
the boys and girls in his arms, and when all
of these had been surrendered, Don Lope
begged them to make peace, giving them
the strongest promises for their safety.
They told him to go away, as they did not

wish to trust themselves to people who had no regard for friendship or their own word which they had pledged. As he seemed unwilling to go away, one of them put an arrow in his bow ready to shoot, and threatened to shoot him with it unless he went off, and they warned him to put on his helmet, but he was unwilling to do so, saying that they would not hurt him as long as he stayed there. When the Indian saw that he did not want to go away, he shot and planted his arrow between the fore feet of the horse, and then put another arrow in his bow and repeated that if he did not go away he would really shoot him. Don Lope put on his helmet and slowly rode back to where the horsemen were, without receiving any harm from them. When they saw that he was really in safety, they began to shoot arrows in showers, with loud yells and cries. The general did not want to make an assault that day, in order to see if they could be brought in some way to make peace, which they would not consider.

Fifteen days later they decided to leave the village one night, and did so, taking the women in their midst. They started about the fourth watch, in the very early morning, on the side where the cavalry was. The alarm was given by those in the camp of Don Rodrigo Maldonado. The enemy attacked them and killed one Spaniard and a horse and wounded others, but they were driven back with great slaughter until they came to the river, where the water flowed swiftly and very cold. They threw themselves into this, and as the men had come quickly from the whole camp to assist the cavalry, there were few who escaped being killed or wounded. Some men from the camp went across the river next day and found many of them who had been overcome by the great cold. They brought these back, cured them, and made servants of them. This ended that siege, and the town was captured, although there were a few who remained in one part of the town and were captured a few days later.

Two captains, Don Diego de Guevara and Juan de Saldivar, had captured the other large village after a siege. Having started out very early one morning to make an ambuscade in which to catch some warriors who used to come out every morning to try to frighten our camp, the spies, who had been placed where they could see when they were coming, saw the people come out and proceed toward the country. The soldiers left the ambuscade and went to the village and saw the people fleeing. They pursued and killed large numbers of them. At the same time those in the camp were ordered to go over the town, and they plundered it, making prisoners of all the people who were found in it, amounting to about a hundred women and children. This siege ended the

last of March, in the year '42.[1] Other
things had happened in the meantime, which
would have been noticed, but that it would
have cut the thread. I have omitted them,
but will relate them now, so that it will be
possible to understand what follows.

CHAPTER XVII

Of how messengers reached the army from the
valley of Señora and how Captain Melchior Diaz
died on the expedition to the Firebrand river.

WE have already related how Captain
Melchior Diaz crossed the Firebrand river
on rafts, in order to continue his discoveries
farther in that direction. About the time
the siege ended, messengers reached the
army from the city of San Hieronimo with
letters from Diego de Alarcon,[1] who had remained there in the place of Melchior Diaz.
These contained the news that Melchior
Diaz had died while he was conducting his
search, and that the force had returned without finding any of the things they were after.
It all happened in this fashion:

After they had crossed the river they continued their search for the coast, which here
turned back toward the south, or between
south and east, because that arm of the sea

[1] Professor Haynes corrected the error in a note in
Winsor's Narrative and Critical History, vol. ii., p.
491, saying that "it is evident that the siege must
have been concluded early in 1541."

[2] Should be Alcaraz.

enters the land due north and this river, which brings its waters down from the north, flowing toward the south, enters the head of the gulf. Continuing in the direction they had been going, they came to some sand banks of hot ashes which it was impossible to cross without being drowned as in the sea. The ground they were standing on trembled like a sheet of paper, so that it seemed as if there were lakes underneath them. It seemed wonderful and like something infernal, for the ashes to bubble up here in several places. After they had gone away from this place, on account of the danger they seemed to be in and of the lack of water, one day a greyhound belonging to one of the soldiers chased some sheep which they were taking along for food. When the captain noticed this, he threw his lance at the dog while his horse was running, so that it stuck up in the ground, and not being able to stop his horse he went over the lance so that it nailed him through the thighs and the iron came out behind, rupturing his bladder. After this the soldiers turned back with their captain, having to fight every day with the Indians, who had remained hostile. He lived about twenty days, during which they proceeded with great difficulty on account of the necessity of carrying him. They returned in good order without losing a man, until he died, and after that they were relieved of the greatest difficulty. When they reached Señora, Alcaraz dispatched the messengers already referred to, so that the general might know of this and also that some of the soldiers were ill disposed and had caused several mutinies, and that he had sentenced two of them to the gallows, but they had afterward escaped from the prison.

When the general learned this, he sent Don Pedro de Tovar to that city to sift out some of the men. He was accompanied by messengers whom the general sent to Don Antonio de Mendoza the viceroy, with an account of what had occurred and with the good news given by the Turk. When Don Pedro de Tovar arrived there, he found that the natives of that province had killed a soldier with a poisoned arrow, which had made only a very little wound in one hand. Several soldiers went to the place where this happened to see about it, and they were not very well received. Don Pedro de Tovar sent Diego de Alcaraz with a force to seize the chiefs and lords of a village in what they call the Valley of Knaves (de los Vellacos), which is in the hills. After getting there and taking these men prisoners, Diego de Alcaraz decided to let them go in exchange for some thread and cloth and other things which the soldiers needed. Finding themselves free, they renewed the war and attacked them, and as they were strong and had poison, they killed several Spaniards and wounded others so that they died on the way back. They retired toward the town, and if they had not had Indian allies from the country of the Hearts, it would have gone worse with them. They got back to the town, leaving 17 soldiers dead from the poison. They would die in agony from only a small wound, the bodies breaking out with an insupportable pestilential stink. When Don Pedro de Tovar saw the harm done, and as it seemed to them that they could not safely stay in that city, he moved 40 leagues toward Cibola into the valley of Suya, where we will leave them, in order to relate what happened to the general and his army after the siege of Tiguex.

CHAPTER XVIII

Of how the general managed to leave the country in peace so as to go in search of Quivira, where the Turk said there was the most wealth.

DURING the siege of Tiguex the general decided to go to Cicuye and take the governor with him, in order to give him his liberty and to promise them that he would give Whiskers his liberty and leave him in the village, as soon as he should start for Quivira. He was received peacefully when he reached Cicuye, and entered the village with several soldiers. They received their governor with much joy and gratitude. After looking over the village and speaking with the natives he returned to his army, leaving Cicuye at peace, in the hope of getting back their captain Whiskers.

After the siege was ended, as we have already related, he sent a captain to Chia, a fine village with many people, which had sent to offer its submission. It was 4 leagues distant to the west of the river. They found it peaceful and gave it four bronze cannon, which were in poor condition, to take care of. Six gentlemen also went to Quirix, a province with seven villages. At the first village, which had about a hundred inhabitants, the natives fled, not daring to wait for our men; but they headed them off by a short cut, riding at full speed, and then they returned to their houses in the village in perfect safety, and then told the other villagers about it and reassured them. In this way the entire region was reassured, little by little, by the time the ice in the river was broken up and it became possible to ford the river and so to continue the journey. The twelve villages of Tiguex, however, were not repopulated at all during the time the army was there, in spite of every promise of security that could possibly be given to them.

And when the river, which for almost four months had been frozen over so that they crossed the ice on horseback, had thawed out, orders were given for the start for Quivira, where the Turk said there was some gold and silver, although not so much as in Arche and the Guaes. There were already some in the army who suspected the Turk, because a Spaniard named Servantes,[1]

[1] Or Cervantes.

who had charge of him during the siege,
solemnly swore that he had seen the Turk
talking with the devil in a pitcher of water,
and also that while he had him under lock
so that no one could speak to him, the Turk
had asked him what Christians had been
killed by the people at Tiguex. He told
him "nobody," and then the Turk answered:
"You lie; five Christians are dead, including a captain." And as Cervantes knew
that he told the truth, he confessed it so as
to find out who had told him about it, and
the Turk said he knew it all by himself and
that he did not need to have anyone tell him
in order to know it. And it was on account
of this that he watched him and saw him
speaking to the devil in the pitcher, as I
have said.

While all this was going on, preparations
were being made to start from Tiguex. At
this time people came from Cibola to see the
general, and he charged them to take good
care of the Spaniards who were coming from
Señora with Don Pedro de Tovar. He gave
them letters to give to Don Pedro, informing
him what he ought to do and how he should
go to find the army, and that he would find
letters under the crosses which the army
would put up along the way. The army
left Tiguex on the 5th of May [1] and returned
to Cicuye, which, as I have said, is twenty-

[1] Coronado says, in his letter of October 20th, that
he started April 23d.

five marches, which means leagues, from
there, taking Whiskers with them. Arrived
there, he gave them their captain, who already went about freely with a guard. The
village was very glad to see him, and the
people were peaceful and offered food. The
governor and Whiskers gave the general a
young fellow called Xabe, a native of Quivira, who could give them information about
the country. This fellow said that there
was gold and silver, but not so much of it
as the Turk had said. The Turk, however,
continued to declare that it was as he had
said. He went as a guide, and thus the
army started off from here.

CHAPTER XIX

Of how they started in search of Quivira and of
what happened on the way.

THE army started from Cicuye, leaving
the village at peace and, as it seemed, contented, and under obligations to maintain
the friendship because their governor and
captain had been restored to them. Proceeding toward the plains, which are all on
the other side of the mountains, after four
days' journey they came to a river with a
large, deep current, which flowed down toward Cicuye, and they named this the Cicuye
river.[1] They had to stop here to make a

---

[1] The Rio Pecos.

bridge so as to cross it. It was finished in four days, by much diligence and rapid work, and as soon as it was done the whole army and the animals crossed. After ten days more they came to some settlements of people who lived like Arabs and who are called Querechos in that region. They had seen the cows for two days. These folks live in tents made of the tanned skins of the cows. They travel around near the cows, killing them for food. They did nothing unusual when they saw our army, except to come out of their tents to look at us, after which they came to talk with the advance guard, and asked who we were. The general talked with them, but as they had already talked with the Turk, who was with the advance guard, they agreed with what he had said. That they were very intelligent is evident from the fact that although they conversed by means of signs they made themselves understood so well that there was no need of an interpreter.[1] They said that there was a very large river over toward where the sun came from, and that one could go along this river through an inhabited region for ninety days without a break from settlement to settlement. They said that the first of these settlements was called Haxa, and that the river was more than a

[1] There is an elaborate account of the sign language of the Indians, by Garrick Mallery, in the first annal report of the Bureau of Ethnology, 1879-80.

league wide and that there were many canoes on it. These folks started off from
here next day with a lot of dogs which
dragged their possessions.

For two days, during which the army
marched in the same direction as that in
which they had come from the settlements
—that is, between north and east, but more
toward the north—they saw other roaming
Querechos and such great numbers of cows
that it already seemed something incredible.
These people gave a great deal of information
about settlements, all toward the east from
where we were. Here Don Garcia broke his
arm and a Spaniard got lost who went off
hunting so far that he was unable to return
to the camp, because the country is very
level. The Turk said it was one or two
days to Haya (Haxa). The general sent
Captain Diego Lopez with ten companions
lightly equipped and a guide to go at full
speed toward the sunrise for two days and
discover Haxa, and then return to meet the
army, which set out in the same direction
next day. They came across so many animals that those who were on the advance
guard killed a large number of bulls. As
these fled they trampled one another in their
haste until they came to a ravine. So many
of the animals fell into this that they filled
it up, and the rest went across on top of
them. The men who were chasing them on
horseback fell in among the animals without
noticing where they were going. Three of

the horses that fell in among the cows, all saddled and bridled, were lost sight of completely.

As it seemed to the general that Diego Lopez ought to be on his way back, he sent six of his companions to follow up the banks of the little river, and as many more down the banks, to look for traces of the horses at the trails to and from the river. It was impossible to find tracks in this country, because the grass straightened up again as soon as it was trodden down. They were found by some Indians from the army who had gone to look for fruit. These got track of them a good league off, and soon came up with them. They followed the river down to the camp, and told the general that in the 20 leagues they had been over they had seen nothing but cows and the sky. There was another native of Quivira with the army, a painted Indian named Ysopete. This Indian had always declared that the Turk was lying, and on account of this the army paid no attention to him, and even now, although he said that the Querechos had consulted with him, Ysopete was not believed.

The general sent Don Rodrigo Maldonado, with his company, forward from here. He traveled four days and reached a large ravine like those of Colima,[1] in the bottom of which he found a large settlement of people. Ca-

[1] The reference is clearly to the district of Colima in western Mexico, where one of the earliest Spanish settlements was made.

beza de Vaca and Dorantes had passed
through this place, so that they presented
Don Rodrigo with a pile of tanned skins and
other things, and a tent as big as a house,
which he directed them to keep until the
army came up. He sent some of his companions to guide the army to that place, so
that they should not get lost, although he
had been making piles of stones and cow
dung for the army to follow. This was the
way in which the army was guided by the
advance guard.

When the general came up with the army
and saw the great quantity of skins, he
thought he would divide them among the
men, and placed guards so that they could
look at them. But when the men arrived
and saw that the general was sending some
of his companions with orders for the guards
to give them some of the skins, and that
these were going to select the best, they
were angry because they were not going to
be divided evenly, and made a rush, and in
less than a quarter of an hour nothing was
left but the empty ground.

The natives who happened to see this
also took a hand in it. The women and
some others were left crying, because they
thought that the strangers were not going to
take anything, but would bless them as Cabeza de Vaca and Dorantes had done when
they passed through here. They found an
Indian girl here who was as white as a Castilian lady, except that she had her chin

painted like a Moorish woman. In general they all paint themselves in this way here, and they decorate their eyes.

CHAPTER XX

Of how great stones fell in the camp, and how they discovered another ravine, where the army was divided into two parts.

WHILE the army was resting in this ravine, as we have related, a tempest came up one afternoon with a very high wind and hail, and in a very short space of time a great quantity of hailstones, as big as bowls, or bigger, fell as thick as raindrops, so that in places they covered the ground two or three spans or more deep. And one hit the horse—or I should say, there was not a horse that did not break away, except two or three which the negroes protected by holding large sea nets over them, with the helmets and shields which all the rest wore; and some of them dashed up on to the sides of the ravine so that they got them down with great difficulty. If this had struck them while they were upon the plain, the army would have been in great danger of being left without its horses, as there were many which they were not able to cover. The hail broke many tents, and battered many helmets, and wounded many of the horses, and broke all the crockery of the army, and the gourds, which was no small loss, because they do not have any crockery in this region. They do not make gourds, nor sow corn, nor eat bread, but instead raw meat—or only half cooked—and fruit.

From here the general sent out to explore the country, and they found another settlement four days from there [1] . . . The country was well inhabited, and they had plenty of kidney beans and prunes like those of Castile, and tall vineyards. These village settlements extended for three days. This was called Cona. Some Teyas,[2] as these people are called, went with the army from here and traveled as far as the end of the other settlements with their packs of dogs and women and children, and then they gave them guides to proceed to a large ravine where the army was. They did not let these guides speak with the Turk and did not receive the same statements from these as they had from the others. These said that Quivira was toward the north, and that we would not find any good road thither. After this they began to believe Ysopete. The ravine which the army had now reached was a league wide from one side to the other, with a little bit of a river at the bottom, and there were many groves of mulberry trees near it, and rosebushes with the same sort

[1] A manera de alixares. The margin reads Alexeres. The word means threshing floor.
[2] Bandelier suggests that the name may have originated in the Indian exclamation, Texia! Texia!—friends! friends!—with which they first greeted the Spaniards.

of fruit that they have in France. They
made verjuice from the unripe grapes at this
ravine, although there were ripe ones.
There were walnuts and the same kind of
fowls as in New Spain, and large quantities
of prunes like those of Castile. During this
journey a Teya was seen to shoot a bull
right through both shoulders with an arrow,
which would be a good shot for a musket.
These people are very intelligent; the women
are well made and modest. They cover
their whole body. They wear shoes and
buskins made of tanned skin. The women
wear cloaks over their small under petticoats,
with sleeves gathered up at the shoulders,
all of skin, and some wore something like
little sanbenitos [1] with a fringe, which
reached half-way down the thigh over the
petticoat.

The army rested several days in this ra-

[1] Capt. John Stevens's New Dictionary says the
sanbenito was "the badge put upon converted Jews
brought out by the Inquisition, being in the nature
of a scapula or a broad piece of cloth hanging before
and behind, with a large Saint Andrews cross on it,
red and yellow. The name corrupted from Saco
Benito, answerable to the sackcloth worn by peni-
tents in the primitive church." Robert Tomson, in
his Voyage into Nova Hispania, 1555, in Hakluyt,
iii., 536, describes his imprisonment by the Holy
Office in the city of Mexico: "We were brought into
the Church, euery one with a S. Benito vpon his
backe, which is a halfe a yard of yellow cloth, with
a hole to put in a mans head in the middest, and cast
ouer a mans head: both flaps hang one before, and
another behinde, and in the middest of euery flap, a
S. Andrewes crosse, made of red cloth, sowed on
vpon the same, and that is called S. Benito."

vine and explored the country. Up to this point they had made thirty-seven days' marches, traveling 6 or 7 leagues a day. It had been the duty of one man to measure and count his steps. They found that it was 250 leagues to the settlements.[1] When the general Francisco Vazquez realized this, and saw that they had been deceived by the Turk heretofore, and as the provisions were giving out and there was no country around here where they could procure more, he called the captains and ensigns together to decide on what they thought ought to be done. They all agreed that the general should go in search of Quivira with thirty horsemen and half a dozen foot-soldiers, and that Don Tristan de Arellano should go back to Tiguex with all the army. When the men in the army learned of this decision, they begged their general not to leave them to conduct the further search, but declared that they all wanted to die with him and did not want to go back. This did not do any good, although the general agreed to send messengers to them within eight days saying whether it was best for them to follow him or not, and with this he set off with the guides he had and with Ysopete. The Turk was taken along in chains.

[1] The Tiguex country is often referred to as the region where the settlements were.

CHAPTER XXI

Of how the army returned to Tiguex and the general reached Quivira.

THE general started from the ravine with the guides that the Teyas had given him. He appointed the alderman Diego Lopez his army-master, and took with him the men who seemed to him to be most efficient, and the best horses. The army still had some hope that the general would send for them, and sent two horsemen, lightly equipped and riding post, to repeat their petition.

The general arrived—I mean, the guides ran away during the first few days and Diego Lopez had to return to the army for guides, bringing orders for the army to return to Tiguex to find food and wait there for the general. The Teyas, as before, willingly furnished him with new guides. The army waited for its messengers and spent a fortnight here, preparing jerked beef to take with them. It was estimated that during this fortnight they killed 500 bulls. The number of these that were there without any cows was something incredible. Many fellows were lost at this time who went out hunting and did not get back to the army for two or three days, wandering about the country as if they were crazy, in one direction or another, not knowing how to get back where they started from, although this

ravine extended in either direction so that
they could find it. Every night they took
account of who was missing, fired guns and
blew trumpets and beat drums and built
great fires, but yet some of them went off so
far and wandered about so much that all this
did not give them any help, although it
helped others. The only way was to go
back where they had killed an animal and
start from there in one direction and another
until they struck the ravine or fell in with
somebody who could put them on the right
road. It is worth noting that the country
there is so level that at midday, after one
has wandered about in one direction and another in pursuit of game, the only thing to
do is to stay near the game quietly until
sunset, so as to see where it goes down, and
even then they have to be men who are
practiced to do it. Those who are not, had
to trust themselves to others.

The general followed his guides until he
reached Quivira, which took forty-eight
days' marching, on acount of the great de-
tour they had made toward Florida. He
was received peacefully on account of the
guides whom he had. They asked the Turk
why he had lied and had guided them so far
out of their way. He said that his country
was in that direction and that, besides this,
the people at Cicuye had asked him to lead
them off on to the plains and lose them, so
that the horses would die when their provisions gave out, and they would be so weak

74

if they ever returned that they would be killed without any trouble, and thus they could take revenge for what had been done to them. This was the reason why he had led them astray, supposing that they did not know how to hunt or to live without corn, while as for the gold, he did not know where there was any of it. He said this like one who had given up hope and who found that he was being persecuted, since they had begun to believe Ysopete, who had guided them better than he had, and fearing lest those who were there might give some advice by which some harm would come to him. They garroted him, which pleased Ysopete very much, because he had always said that Ysopete was a rascal and that he did not know what he was talking about and had always hindered his talking with anybody. Neither gold nor silver nor any trace of either was found among these people. Their lord wore a copper plate on his neck and prized it highly.

The messengers whom the army had sent to the general returned, as I said, and then, as they brought no news except what the alderman had delivered, the army left the ravine and returned to the Teyas, where they took guides who led them back by a more direct road. They readily furnished these, because these people are always roaming over this country in pursuit of the animals and so know it thoroughly. They keep their road in this way: In the morning they notice where the sun rises and observe the direction they are going to take, and then shoot an arrow in this direction. Before reaching this they shoot another over it, and in this way they go all day toward the water where they are to end the day. In this way they covered in 25 days what had taken them 37 days going, besides stopping to hunt cows on the way. They found many salt lakes on this road, and there was a great quantity of salt. There were thick pieces of it on top of the water bigger than tables, as thick as four or five fingers. Two or three spans down under water there was salt which tasted better than that in the floating pieces, because this was rather bitter. It was crystalline. All over these plains there were large numbers of animals like squirrels and a great number of their holes.

On its return the army reached the Cicuye river more than 30 leagues below there—I mean below the bridge they had made when they crossed it, and they followed it up to that place. In general, its banks are covered with a sort of rose bushes, the fruit of which tastes like muscatel grapes. They grow on little twigs about as high up as a man. It has the parsley leaf. There were unripe grapes and currants (?) and wild marjoram. The guides said this river joined that of Tiguex more than 20 days from here, and that its course turned toward the east. It is believed that it flows into the mighty river of the Holy Spirit (Espiritu Santo), which the men with Don Hernando de Soto discovered in Florida. A painted Indian woman ran away from Juan de Saldibar and hid in the ravines about this time, because she recognized the country of Tiguex where she had been a slave. She fell into the hands of some Spaniards who had entered the country from Florida to explore it in this direction. After I got back to New Spain I heard them say that the Indian told them that she had run away from other men like them nine days, and that she gave the names of some captains; from which we ought to believe that we were not far from the region they discovered, although they said they were more than 200 leagues inland. I believe the land at that point is more than 600 leagues across from sea to sea.

As I said, the army followed the river up as far as Cicuye, which it found ready for war and unwilling to make any advances toward peace or to give any food to the army. From there they went on to Tiguex where several villages had been reinhabited, but the people were afraid and left them again.

CHAPTER XXII

Of how the general returned from Quivira and of other expeditions toward the North.

AFTER Don Tristan de Arellano reached Tiguex, about the middle of July, in the year '42,[1] he had provisions collected for the coming winter. Captain Francisco de Barrionuevo was sent up the river toward the north with several men. He saw two provinces, one of which was called Hemes and had seven villages, and the other Yuqueyunque.[2] The inhabitants of Hemes came out peaceably and furnished provisions. At Yuqueyunque the whole nation left two very fine villages which they had on either side of the river entirely vacant, and went into the mountains, where they had four very strong villages in a rough country, where it was impossible for horses to go. In the two villages there was a great deal of food and some very beautiful glazed earthenware with many figures and different shapes. Here they also found many bowls full of a carefully selected shining metal with which they glazed the earthenware. This shows that mines of silver would be found in that country if they should hunt for them.

There was a large and powerful river, I mean village, which was called Braba, 20 leagues farther up the river, which our men called Valladolid.[3] The river flowed through

[1] Castañeda's date is, as usual, a year later than the actual one.
[2] Yuge-uing-ge, as Bandelier spells it, is the aboriginal name of a former Tewa village, the site of which is occupied by the hamlet of Chamita, opposite San Juan. The others are near by.
[3] Taos, or Te-uat-ha. See Bandelier's Final Report, vol. i., p. 123, for the identification of these places.

the middle of it. The natives crossed it by wooden bridges, made of very long, large, squared pines. At this village they saw the largest and finest hot rooms or estufas that there were in the entire country, for they had a dozen pillars, each one of which was twice as large around as one could reach and twice as tall as a man. Hernando de Alvarado visited this village when he discovered Cicuye. The country is very high and very cold. The river is deep and very swift, without any ford. Captain Barrionuevo returned from here, leaving the province at peace.

Another captain went down the river in search of the settlements which the people at Tutahaco had said were several days distant from there. This captain went down 80 leagues and found four large villages which he left at peace. He proceeded until he found that the river sank into the earth, like the Guadiana in Estremadura.[1] He did not go on to where the Indians said that it came out much larger, because his commission did not extend for more than 80 leagues march. After this captain got back, as the time had arrived which the captain had set for his return from Quivira, and as he had not come back, Don Tristan selected 40

[1] This rendering, doubtless correct, is due to Ternaux. The Guadiana, however, reappears above ground some time before it begins to mark the boundary of the Spanish province of Estremadura. The Castañeda family had its seat in quite the other end of the peninsula.

companions and, leaving the army to Francisco de Barrionuevo, he started with them in search of the general.

When he reached Cicuye the people came out of the village to fight, which detained him there four days, while he punished them, which he did by firing some volleys into the village. These killed several men, so that they did not come out against the army, since two of their principal men had been killed on the first day. Just then word was brought that the general was coming, and so Don Tristan had to stay there on this account also, to keep the road open. Everybody welcomed the general on his arrival, with great joy. The Indian Xabe, who was the young fellow who had been given to the general at Cicuye when he started off in search of Quivira, was with Don Tristan de Arellano and when he learned that the general was coming he acted as if he was greatly pleased, and said, "Now when the general comes, you will see that there is gold and silver in Quivira, although not so much as the Turk said." When the general arrived, and Xabe saw that they had not found anything, he was sad and silent, and kept declaring that there was some. He made many believe that it was so, because the general had not dared to enter into the country on account of its being thickly settled and his force not very strong, and that he had returned to lead his army there after the rains, because it had begun to rain there already, as it was early in August when he left. It took him forty days to return, traveling lightly equipped. The Turk had said when they left Tiguex that they ought not to load the horses with too much provisions, which would tire them so that they could not afterward carry the gold and silver, from which it is very evident that he was deceiving them.

The general reached Cicuye with his force and at once set off for Tiguex, leaving the village more quiet, for they had met him peaceably and had talked with him. When he reached Tiguex, he made his plans to pass the winter there, so as to return with the whole army, because it was said that he brought information regarding large settlements and very large rivers, and that the country was very much like that of Spain in the fruits and vegetation and seasons. They were not ready to believe that there was no gold there, but instead had suspicions that there was some farther back in the country, because, although this was denied, they knew what the thing was and had a name for it among themselves—acochis. With this we end this first part, and now we will give an account of the provinces.

SECOND PART

Which Treats of the High Villages and Provinces and of their Habits and Customs, as Collected by Pedro de Castañeda, Native of the City of Najara.

Laus Deo.

It does not seem to me that the reader will be satisfied with having seen and understood what I have already related about the expedition, although that has made it easy to see the difference between the report which told about vast treasures, and the places where nothing like this was either found or known. It is to be noted that in place of settlements great deserts were found, and instead of populous cities villages of 200 inhabitants and only 800 or 1,000 people in the largest. I do not know whether this will furnish grounds for pondering and considering the uncertainty of this life. To please these, I wish to give a detailed account of all the inhabited region seen and discovered by this expedition, and some of their ceremonies and habits, in accordance with what we came to know about them, and the limits within which each province falls, so that hereafter it may be possible to understand in what direction Florida lies and in what direction Greater India; and this land of New Spain is part of the mainland with Peru, and with Greater India or China as well, there not being any strait between to separate them. On the other hand, the country is so wide that there is room for these vast deserts which lie between the two seas, for the coast of the North sea beyond Florida stretches toward the Bacallaos [1] and then turns toward Norway, while that of the South sea turns toward the west, making another bend down toward the south almost like a bow and stretches away toward India, leaving room for the lands that border on the mountains on both sides to stretch out in such a way as to have between them these great plains which are full of cattle and many other animals of different sorts, since they are not inhabited, as I will relate farther on. There is every sort of game and fowl there, but no snakes, for they are free from these. I will leave the account of the return of the army to New Spain until I have shown what slight occasion there was for this. We will begin our account with the city of Culiacan, and point out the differences between the one country and the other, on account of which one ought to be settled by Spaniards and the other not. It should be the reverse, however, with Christians,

[1] The Newfoundland region.

since there are intelligent men in one, and in the other wild animals and worse than beasts.

CHAPTER I

Of the province of Culiacan and of its habits and customs.

CULIACAN is the last place in the New Kingdom of Galicia, and was the first settlement made by Nuño de Guzman when he conquered this kingdom. It is 210 leagues west of Mexico. In this province there are three chief languages, besides other related dialects. The first is that of the Tahus, who are the best and most intelligent race. They are now the most settled and have received the most light from the faith. They worship idols and make presents to the devil of their goods and riches, consisting of cloth and turquoises. They do not eat human flesh nor sacrifice it. They are accustomed to keep very large snakes, which they venerate. Among them there are men dressed like women who marry other men and serve as their wives. At a great festival they consecrate the women who wish to live unmarried, with much singing and dancing, at which all the chiefs of the locality gather and dance naked, and after all have danced with her they put her in a hut that has been decorated for this event and the chiefs adorn her with clothes and bracelets of fine turquoises, and then the chiefs go in one by one to lie with her, and all the others who wish, follow them. From this time on these women can not refuse anyone who pays them a certain amount agreed on for this. Even if they take husbands, this does not exempt them from obliging anyone who pays them. The greatest festivals are on market days. The custom is for the husbands to buy the women whom they marry, of their fathers and relatives at a high price, and then to take them to a chief, who is considered to be a priest, to deflower them and see if she is a virgin; and if she is not, they have to return the whole price, and he can keep her for his wife or not, or let her be consecrated, as he chooses. At these times they all get drunk.

The second language is that of the Pacaxes, the people who live in the country between the plains and the mountains. These people are more barbarous. Some of them who live near the mountains eat human flesh. They are great sodomites, and have many wives, even when these are sisters. They worship painted and sculptured stones, and are much given to witchcraft and sorcery.

The third language is that of the Acaxes, who are in possession of a large part of the hilly country and all of the mountains. They go hunting for men just as they hunt animals. They all eat human flesh, and he who has the most human bones and skulls hung up around his house is most feared and respected. They live in settlements and in very rough country, avoiding the plains. In passing from one settlement to another, there is always a ravine in the way which they can not cross, although they can talk together across it. At the slightest call 500 men collect, and on any pretext kill and eat one another. Thus it has been very hard to subdue these people, on account of the roughness of the country, which is very great.

Many rich silver mines have been found in this country. They do not run deep, but soon give out. The gulf of the sea begins on the coast of this province, entering the land 250 leagues toward the north and ending at the mouth of the Firebrand (Tizon) river. This country forms its eastern limit, and California the western. From what I have been told by men who had navigated it, it is 30 leagues across from point to point, because they lose sight of this country when they see the other. They say the gulf is over 150 leagues broad (or deep), from shore to shore. The coast makes a turn toward the south at the Firebrand river, bending down to California, which turns toward the west, forming that peninsula which was formerly held to be an island, because it was a low sandy country. It is inhabited by brutish, bestial, naked people who eat their own offal. The men and women couple like animals, the female openly getting down on all fours.

CHAPTER II

Of the province of Petlatlan and all the inhabited country as far as Chichilticalli.

PETLATLAN is a settlement of houses covered with a sort of mats made of *plants*. These are collected into villages, extending along a river from the mountains to the sea. The people are of the same race and habits as the Culuacanian Tahues. There is much sodomy among them. In the mountain district there is a large population and more settlements. These people have a somewhat different language from the Tahues, although they understand each other. It is called Petlatlan because the houses are made of petates or palm-leaf mats.[1] Houses of this sort are found for more than 240 leagues in this region, to the beginning of the Cibola wilderness. The nature of the country changes here very greatly, because from this point on there are no trees except the pine, nor are there any fruits except a few tunas,[2] mesquites,[3] and pitahayas.[4]

Petlatlan is 20 leagues from Culiacan, and

[1] Bandelier found the Opata Indians living in houses made with "a slight foundation of cobblestones which supported a framework of posts standing in a thin wall of rough stones and mud, while a slanting roof of yucca or palm leaves covered the whole."—Final Report, pt. i., p. 58.

[2] The *Opuntia tuna* or prickly pear.

[3] *Prosopis juliflora.*   [4] *Cereus thurberii.*

it is 130 leagues from here to the valley of Señora. There are many rivers between the two, with settlements of the same sort of people—for example, Sinoloa, Boyomo, Teocomo, Yaquimi, and other smaller ones. There is also the Corazones or Hearts, which is in our possession, down the valley of Señora.[1]

Señora is a river and valley thickly settled by able-bodied people. The women wear petticoats of tanned deerskin, and little san benitos reaching half way down the body. The chiefs of the villages go up on some little heights they have made for this purpose, like public criers, and there make proclamations for the space of an hour, regulating those things they have to attend to. They have some little huts for shrines, all over the outside of which they stick many arrows, like a hedgehog. They do this when they are eager for war. All about this province toward the mountains there is a large population in separate little provinces containing ten or twelve villages. Seven or eight of them, of which I know the names, are Comupatrico, Mochilagua, Arispa, and the Little Valley. There are others which we did not see.

It is 40 leagues from Señora to the valley of Suya. The town of Saint Jerome (San Hieronimo) was established in this valley, where there was a rebellion later, and part

[1] Sonora.

of the people who had settled there were killed, as will be seen in the third part. There are many villages in the neighborhood of this valley. The people are the same as those in Señora and have the same dress and language, habits, and customs, like all the rest as far as the desert of Chichilticalli. The women paint their chins and eyes like the Moorish women of Barbary. They are great sodomites. They drink wine made of the pitahaya, which is the fruit of a great thistle which opens like the pomegranate. The wine makes them stupid. They make a great quantity of preserves from the tuna; they preserve it in a large amount of its sap without other honey. They make bread of the mesquite, like cheese, which keeps good for a whole year.[1] There are native melons in this country so large that a person can carry only one of them. They cut these into slices and dry them in the sun. They are good to eat, and taste like figs, and are better than dried meat; they are very good and sweet, keeping for a whole year when prepared in this way.[2]

In this country there were also tame

---

[1] Bandelier, Final Report, pt. i., p. 111, quotes from the Relaciones of Zárate-Salmeron, of some Arizona Indians: "Tambien tienen para su sustento Mescali que es conserva de raiz de maguey." The strong liquor is made from the root of the Mexican or American agave.

[2] These were doubtless cantaloupes. The southwestern Indians still slice and dry them in a manner similar to that here described.

eagles, which the chiefs esteemed to be something fine.[1] No fowls of any sort were seen in any of these villages except in this valley of Suya, where fowls like those of Castile were found. Nobody could find out how they came to be so far inland, the people being all at war with one another. Between Suya and Chichilticalli there are many sheep and mountain goats with very large bodies and horns. Some Spaniards declare that they have seen flocks of more than a hundred together, which ran so fast that they disappeared very quickly.

At Chichilticalli the country changes its character again and the spiky vegetation ceases. The reason is that the gulf reaches as far up as this place, and the mountain chain changes its direction at the same time that the coast does. Here they had to cross and pass through the mountains in order to get into the level country.

CHAPTER III

Of Chichilticalli and the desert, of Cibola, its customs and habits, and of other things.

CHICHILTICALLI is so called because the friars found a house at this place which was formerly inhabited by people who separated from Cibola. It was made of colored or red-

[1] The Pueblo Indians, particularly the Zuñi and Hopi, keep eagles for their feathers, which are highly prized because of their reputed sacred character.

THE JOURNEY OF CORONADO

dish earth.[1] The house was large and appeared to have been a fortress. It must have been destroyed by the people of the district, who are the most barbarous people that have yet been seen. They live in separate cabins and not in settlements. They live by hunting. The rest of the country is all wilderness, covered with pine forests. There are great quantities of the pine nuts. The pines are two or three times as high as a man before they send out branches. There is a sort of oak with sweet acorns, of which they make cakes like sugar plums with dried coriander seeds. It is very sweet, like sugar. Watercress grows in many springs, and there are rosebushes, and pennyroyal, and wild marjoram.

There are barbels and picones, like those of Spain, in the rivers of this wilderness. Gray lions and leopards were seen.[2] The country rises continually from the beginning of the wilderness until Cibola is reached, which is 85 leagues, going north. From Culiacan to the edge of the wilderness the route had kept the north on the left hand.

Cibola[3] is seven villages. The largest is

[1] Chichiltic-calli, a red object or house, according to Molina's Vocabulario Mexicano, 1555. Bandelier, Historical Introduction, p. 11, gives references to the ancient and modern descriptions.

[2] These were evidently the mountain lion and the wild-cat.

[3] Albert S. Gatschet, in his Zwölf Sprachen, p. 106, says that this word is now to be found only in the dialect of the pueblo of Isleta, under the form sibúlodá, buffalo.

called Maçaque.[1] The houses are ordinarily
three or four stories high, but in Maçaque
there are houses with four and seven stories.
These people are very intelligent. They
cover their privy parts and all the immodest
parts with cloths made like a sort of table
napkin, with fringed edges and a tassel at
each corner, which they tie over the hips.
They wear long robes of feathers and of the
skins of hares and cotton blankets.[2] The
women wear blankets, which they tie or
knot over the left shoulder, leaving the right
arm out. These serve to cover the body.
They wear a neat well-shaped outer garment
of skin. They gather their hair over the
two ears, making a frame which looks like
an old-fashioned headdress.[3]

[1] Matsaki, the ruins of which are at the northwestern base of Thunder mountain. See Bandelier's
Final Report, pt. i., p. 133, and Hodge, First Discovered City of Cibola.

[2] The mantles of rabbit hair are still worn at Moki,
but those of turkey plumes are out of use altogether.
See Bandelier's Final Report, pt. i., pp. 37 and 158.
They used also the fiber of the yucca and agave for
making clothes.

[3] J. G. Owens, Hopi Natal Ceremonies, in Journal
of American Archæology and Ethnology, vol. ii., p.
165 n., says: " The dress of the Hopi [Moki, or Tusay-
an] women consists of a black blanket about 3½ feet
square, folded around the body from the left side.
It passes under the left arm and over the right
shoulder, being sewed together on the right side,
except a hole about 3 inches long near the upper
end through which the arm is thrust. This is belted
in at the waist by a sash about 3 inches wide. Sometimes, though not frequently, a shirt is worn under
this garment, and a piece of muslin, tied together by
two adjacent corners, is usually near by, to be thrown

This country is in a valley between mountains in the form of isolated cliffs. They cultivate the corn, which does not grow very high, in patches. There are three or four large fat ears having each eight hundred grains on every stalk growing upward from the ground, something not seen before in these parts. There are large numbers of bears in this province, and lions, wild-cats, deer, and otter. There are very fine turquoises, although not so many as was reported. They collect the pine nuts each year, and store them up in advance. A man does not have more than one wife. There are estufas or hot rooms in the villages, which are the courtyards or places where they gather for consultation. They do not have chiefs as in New Spain, but are ruled by a council of the oldest men. They have priests who preach to them, whom they call papas.[1] These are the elders. They go up on the highest roof of the village and preach to the village from there, like public criers, in the morning while the sun is rising, the whole village being silent and sitting in the galleries to listen.[2] They tell them how

over the shoulders. Most of the women have moccasins, which they put on at certain times."

[1] Papa in the Zuñi language signifies "elder brother," and may allude either to age or to rank.

[2] Dr. J. Walter Fewkes, in his Few Summer Ceremonials at the Tusayan Pueblos, p. 7, describes the Dä'wä-wýmp-ki-yas, a small number of priests of the sun. Among other duties, they pray to the rising sun, whose course they are said to watch, and they prepare offerings to it.

they are to live, and I believe that they give
certain commandments for them to keep, for
there is no drunkenness among them nor
sodomy nor sacrifices, neither do they eat
human flesh nor steal, but they are usually
at work. The estufas belong to the whole
village. It is a sacrilege for the women to
go into the estufas to sleep.[1] They make
the cross as a sign of peace. They burn
their dead, and throw the implements used
in their work into the fire with the bodies.[2]

[1] In his Few Summer Ceremonials at Tusayan, p.
6, Dr. Fewkes says that "with the exception of their
own dances, women do not take part in the secret
kibva [estufa] ceremonials; but it can not be said
that they are debarred entrance as assistants in making the paraphernalia of the dances, or when they
are called upon to represent dramatizations of tra-
ditions in which women figure."

[2] Mr. Frank Hamilton Cushing, in the Compte-
rendu of the Congrès International des Americani-
istes, Berlin, 1888, pp. 171–172, speaking of the excavations of "Los Muertos" in southern Arizona, says:
"All the skeletons, especially of adults [in the
intramural burials], were, with but few exceptions,
disposed with the heads to the east and slightly
elevated as though resting on pillows, so as to face
the west; and the hands were usually placed at the
sides or crossed over the breast. With nearly all
were paraphernalia, household utensils, articles of
adornment, etc. This paraphernalia quite invariably partook of a sacerdotal character." In the
pyral mounds outside the communal dwellings,
"each burial consisted of a vessel, large or small,
according to the age of the person whose thoroughly
cremated remains it was designed to receive, together, ordinarily, with traces of the more valued
and smaller articles of personal property sacrificed
at the time of cremation. Over each such vessel
was placed either an inverted bowl or a cover
(roughly rounded by chipping) of potsherds, which
latter, in most cases, showed traces of having been

It is 20 leagues to Tusayan, going north-west. This is a province with seven villages, of the same sort, dress, habits, and ceremonies as at Cibola. There may be as many as 3,000 or 4,000 men in the fourteen villages of these two provinces. It is 40 leagues or more to Tiguex, the road trending

firmly cemented, by means of mud plaster, to the vessels they covered. Again, around each such burial were found always from two or three to ten or a dozen broken vessels, often, indeed, a complete set; namely, eating and drinking bowls, water-jar and bottle, pitcher, spheroidal food receptacle, ladles large and small, and cooking-pot. Sometimes, however, one or another of these vessels actually designed for sacrifice with the dead, was itself used as the receptacle of his or her remains. In every such case the vessel had been either punctured at the bottom or on one side, or else violently cracked —from Zuñi customs, in the process of ' killing ' it." The remains of other articles were around, burned in the same fire.

Since the above note was extracted, excavations have been conducted by Dr. J. Walter Fewkes at the prehistoric Hopi pueblo of Sikyatki, an exhaustive account of which will be published in a forthcoming report of the Bureau of Ethnology. Sikyatki is located at the base of the First Mesa of Tusayan, about 3 miles from Hano. The house structures were situated on an elongated elevation, the western extremity of the village forming a sort of acropolis. On the northern, western, and southern slopes of the height, outside the village proper, cemeteries were found, and in these most of the excavations were conducted. Many graves were uncovered at a depth varying from 1 foot to 10 feet, but the skeletons were in such condition as to be practically beyond recovery. Accompanying these remains were hundreds of food and water vessels in great variety of form and decoration, and in quality of texture far better than any earthenware previously recovered from a pueblo people. With the remains of the priests there were found, in addi-

toward the north. The rock of Acuco, which we described in the first part, is between these.

CHAPTER IV

Of how they live at Tiguex, and of the province of Tiguex and its neighborhood.

TIGUEX is a province with twelve villages on the banks of a large, swift river; some villages on one side and some on the other. It is a spacious valley two leagues wide, and a very high, rough, snow-covered mountain chain lies east of it. There are seven villages in the ridges at the foot of this— four on the plain and three situated on the skirts of the mountain.

There are seven villages 7 leagues to the north [*i.e.* of Tiguex], at Quirix, and the seven villages of the province of Hemes are 40 leagues northeast. It is four leagues north or east to Acha.[1] Tutahaco, a province with eight villages, is toward the southeast. In general, these villages all have the same

tion to the usual utensils, terra cotta and stone pipes, beads, prayer-sticks, quartz crystals, arrowpoints, stone and shell fetiches, sacred paint, and other paraphernalia similar to that used by the Hopi of today. The house walls were constructed of small, flat stones brought from the neighboring mesa, laid in adobe mortar and plastered with the same material. The rooms were invariably small, averaging perhaps 8 feet square, and the walls were quite thin. No human remains were found in the houses, nor were any evidences of cremation observed.

[1] The pueblo of Picuris.

habits and customs, although some have
some things in particular which the others
have not.[1] They are governed by the opinions of the elders. They all work together
to build the villages, the women being engaged in making the mixture and the walls,
while the men bring the wood and put it in
place.[2] They have no lime, but they make
a mixture of ashes, coals, and dirt which is
almost as good as mortar, for when the house
is to have four stories, they do not make the
walls more than half a yard thick. They
gather a great pile of twigs of thyme and

[1] Bandelier gives a general account of the internal
condition of the Pueblo Indians, with references to
the older Spanish writers, in his Final Report, pt. i.,
p. 135.
[2] Lewis H. Morgan, in his Ruins of a Stone Pueblo, Peabody Museum Reports, vol. xii., p. 541,
says: "Adobe is a kind of pulverized clay with a
bond of considerable strength by mechanical cohe-
sion. In southern Colorado, in Arizona, and New
Mexico there are immense tracts covered with what
is called adobe soil. It varies somewhat in the degree of its excellence. The kind of which they
make their pottery has the largest per cent. of alu-
mina, and its presence is indicated by the salt weed
which grows in this particular soil. This kind also
makes the best adobe mortar. The Indians use it
freely in laying their walls, as freely as our masons
use lime mortar; and although it never acquires the
hardness of cement, it disintegrates slowly. . . .
This adobe mortar is adapted only to the dry climate of southern Colorado, Arizona, and New Mexico, where the precipitation is less than 5 inches
per annum. . . . To the presence of this adobe soil,
found in such abundance in the regions named, and
to the sandstone of the bluffs, where masses are
often found in fragments, we must attribute the
great progress made by these Indians in house
building."

sedge grass and set it afire, and when it is
half coals and ashes they throw a quantity
of dirt and water on it and mix it all together. They make round balls of this,
which they use instead of stones after they
are dry, fixing them with the same mixture,
which comes to be like a stiff clay. Before
they are married the young men serve the
whole village in general, and fetch the wood
that is needed for use, putting it in a pile in
the courtyard of the villages, from which
the women take it to carry to their houses.

The young men live in the estufas, which
are in the yards of the village.[1] They are
underground, square or round, with pine pillars. Some were seen with twelve pillars and
with four in the center as large as two men
could stretch around. They usually had
three or four pillars. The floor was made of
large, smooth stones, like the baths which
they have in Europe. They have a hearth
made like the binnacle or compass box of a
ship, in which they burn a handful of

[1] Bandelier discusses the estufas in his Final Report, pt. i., p. 144 ff., giving quotations from the
Spanish writers, with his usual wealth of footnotes.
Dr. Fewkes, in his Zuñi Summer Ceremonials, says:
"These rooms are semisubterranean (in Zuñi), situated on the first or ground floor, never, so far as I
have seen, on the second or higher stories. They
are rectangular or square rooms, built of stone, with
openings just large enough to admit the head serving as windows, and still preserve the old form of
entrance by ladders through a sky hole in the roof.
Within, the estufas have bare walls and are unfur-
nished, but have a raised ledge about the walls,
serving as seats."

thyme at a time to keep up the heat, and they can stay in there just as in a bath. The top was on a level with the ground. Some that were seen were large enough for a game of ball. When any man wishes to marry, it has to be arranged by those who govern. The man has to spin and weave a blanket and place it before the woman, who covers herself with it and becomes his wife. The houses belong to the women, the estufas to the men. If a man repudiates his woman, he has to go to the estufa. It is forbidden for women to sleep in the estufas, or to enter these for any purpose except to give their husbands or sons something to eat. The men spin and weave. The women bring up the children and prepare the food. The country is so fertile that they do not have to break up the ground the year round, but only have to sow the seed, which is presently covered by the fall of snow, and the ears come up under the snow. In one year they gather enough for seven. A very large number of cranes and wild geese and crows and starlings live on what is sown, and for all this, when they come to sow for another year, the fields are covered with corn which they have not been able to finish gathering.

There are a great many native fowl in these provinces, and cocks with great hanging chins.[1] When dead, these keep for sixty days, and longer in winter, without losing

---

[1] The American turkey cocks.

their feathers or opening, and without any bad smell, and the same is true of dead men.

The villages are free from nuisances, because they go outside to excrete, and they pass their water into clay vessels, which they empty at a distance from the village.[1]

They keep the separate houses where they prepare the food for eating and where they grind the meal, very clean. This is a separate room or closet, where they have a trough with three stones fixed in stiff clay. Three women go in here, each one having a stone, with which one of them breaks the corn, the next grinds it, and the third grinds it again.[2]

---

[1] A custom still common at Zuñi and other pueblos. Before the introduction of manufactured dyes the Hopi used urine as a mordant.

[2] Mr. Owens, in the Journal of American Ethnology and Archæology, vol. ii., p. 163 *n*., describes these mealing troughs· "In every house will be found a trough about 6 feet long, 2 feet wide, and 8 inches deep, divided into three or more compartments. In the older houses the sides and partitions are made of stone slabs, but in some of the newer ones they are made of boards. Within each compartment is a stone (trap rock preferred) about 18 inches long and a foot wide, set in a bed of adobe and inclined at an angle of about 35°. This is not quite in the center of the compartment, but is set about inches 3 nearer the right side than the left, and its higher edge is against the edge of the trough. This constitutes the nether stone of the mill. The upper stone is about 14 inches long, 3 inches wide, and varies in thickness according to the fineness of the meal desired. The larger stone is called a máta and the smaller one a matáki. The woman places the corn in the trough, then kneels behind it and grasps the matáki in both hands. This she slides, by a motion from the back, back and forth over the máta. At intervals she re-

They take off their shoes, do up their hair, shake their clothes, and cover their heads before they enter the door. A man sits at the door playing on a fife while they grind, moving the stones to the music and singing together. They grind a large quantity at one time, because they make all their bread of meal soaked in warm water, like wafers. They gather a great quantity of brushwood and dry it to use for cooking all through the year. There are no fruits good to eat in the country, except the pine nuts. They have their preachers. Sodomy is not found among them. They do not eat human flesh nor make sacrifices of it. The people are not cruel, for they had Francisco de Ovando in Tiguex about forty days, after he was dead, and when the village was captured, he was found among their dead, whole and without any other wound except the one which killed him, white as snow, without any bad smell. I found out several things about them from one of our Indians, who had been a captive among them for a whole year. I asked him especially for the reason why the young women in that province went entirely naked,

leases her hold with her left hand and with it places the material to be ground upon the upper end of the máta. She usually sings in time to her grinding motion."

There is a more extended account of these troughs in Mindeleff's Pueblo Architecture, in the Eighth Report of the Bureau of Ethnology, p. 208. This excellent monograph, with its wealth of illustrations, is an invaluable introduction to any study of the southwestern village Indians.

however cold it might be, and he told me that the virgins had to go around this way until they took a husband, and that they covered themselves after they had known man. The men here wear little shirts of tanned deerskin and their long robes over this. In all these provinces they have earthenware glazed with antimony and jars of extraordinary labor and workmanship, which were worth seeing.[1]

CHAPTER V

Of Cicuye and the villages in its neighborhood, and of how some people came to conquer this country.

WE have already said that the people of Tiguex and of all the provinces on the banks of that river were all alike, having the same ways of living and the same customs. It will not be necessary to say anything particular about them. I wish merely to give an account of Cicuye and some depopulated villages which the army saw on the direct road which it followed thither, and of others that were across the snowy mountains near Tiguex, which also lay in that region above the river.

[1] See W. H. Holmes, Pottery of the Ancient Pueblos, Fourth Annual Report of the Bureau of Ethnology; also his Illustrated Catalogue of a portion of the collections made during the field season of 1881, in the Third Annual Report.

Cicuye [1] is a village of nearly five hundred warriors, who are feared throughout that country. It is square, situated on a rock, with a large court or yard in the middle, containing the estufas. The houses are all alike, four stories high. One can go over the top of the whole village without there being a street to hinder. There are corridors going all around it at the first two stories, by which one can go around the whole village. These are like outside balconies, and they are able to protect themselves under these. The houses do not have doors below, but they use ladders, which can be lifted up like a drawbridge, and so go up to the corridors which are on the inside of the village. As the doors of the houses open on the corridor of that story, the corridor serves as a street. The houses that open on the plain are right back of those that open on the court, and in time of war they go through those behind them. The village is inclosed by a low wall of stone. There is a spring of water inside, which they are able to divert. [2] The people of this village boast that no one has been able to conquer them and that they conquer whatever villages they

[1] Bandelier, in his Visit to Pecos, p. 114, n., states that the former name of the pueblo was Âquin, and suggests the possibility of Castañeda having originally written Acuyé. The Relacion del Suceso has Acuique.

[2] The spring was "still trickling out beneath a massive ledge of rocks on the west sill" when Bandelier sketched it in 1880.

wish. The people and their customs are like those of the other villages. Their virgins also go nude until they take husbands, because they say that if they do anything wrong then it will be seen, and so they do not do it. They do not need to be ashamed because they go around as they were born.

There is a village, small and strong, between Cicuye and the province of Quirix, which the Spaniards named Ximena,[1] and another village almost deserted, only one part of which is inhabited.[2] This was a large village, and judging from its condition and newness it appeared to have been destroyed. They called this the village of the granaries or silos, because large underground cellars were found here stored with corn. There was another large village farther on, entirely destroyed and pulled down, in the yards of which there were many stone balls, as big as 12-quart bowls, which seemed to have been thrown by engines or catapults, which had destroyed the village. All that I was able to find out about them was that, sixteen years before, some people called Teyas,[3] had

[1] The former Tano pueblo of Galisteo, a mile and a half northeast of the present town of the same name, in Santa Fé county.

[2] According to Mota Padilla, this was called Coquite.

[3] These Indians were seen by Coronado during his journey across the plains. As Mr. Hodge has suggested, they may have been the Comanches, who on many occasions are known to have made inroads on the pueblo of Pecos.

come to this country in great numbers and
had destroyed these villages. They had besieged Cicuye but had not been able to capture it, because it was strong, and when they
left the region, they had made peace with
the whole country. It seems as if they must
have been a powerful people, and that they
must have had engines to knock down the
villages. The only thing they could tell
about the direction these people came from
was by pointing toward the north. They
usually call these people Teyas or brave
men, just as the Mexicans say chichimecas
or braves, for the Teyas whom the army
saw were brave. These knew the people in
the settlements, and were friendly with them,
and they (the Teyas of the plains) went there
to spend the winter under the wings of the
settlements. The inhabitants do not dare
to let them come inside, because they can
not trust them. Although they are received
as friends, and trade with them, they do
not stay in the villages over night, but
outside under the wings. The villages are
guarded by sentinels with trumpets, who
call to one another just as in the fortresses
of Spain.

There are seven other villages along this
route, toward the snowy mountains, one of
which has been half destroyed by the people
already referred to. These were under the
rule of Cicuye. Cicuye is in a little valley
between mountain chains and mountains
covered with large pine forests. There is a

little stream which contains very good trout and otters, and there are very large bears and good falcons hereabouts.

CHAPTER VI

Which gives the number of villages which were seen in the country of the terraced houses, and their population.

BEFORE I proceed to speak of the plains, with the cows and settlements and tribes there, it seems to me that it will be well for the reader to know how large the settlements were, where the houses with stories, gathered into villages, were seen, and how great an extent of country they occupied.[1] As I say, Cibola is the first:

Cibola, seven villages.

Tusayan, seven villages.

The rock of Acuco, one.

Tiguex, twelve villages.

Tutahaco, eight villages.

These villages were below the river.

Quirix,[2] seven villages.

[1] Bandelier, Final Report, pt. i., p. 34. "With the exception of Acoma, there is not a single pueblo standing where it was at the time of Coronado, or even sixty years later, when Juan de Oñate accomplished the peaceable reduction of the New Mexican village Indians." Compare with the discussion in this part of his Final Report, Mr. Bandelier's attempt to identify the various clusters of villages, in his Historical Introduction, pp. 22–24.

[2] The Queres district, now represented by Santo Domingo, San Felipe, Santa Ana, Sia (Castañeda's

In the snowy mountains, seven villages.

Ximena,[1] three villages.

Cicuye, one village.

Hemes,[2] seven villages.

Aguas Calientes,[2] or Boiling Springs, three villages.

Yuqueyunque,[3] in the mountains, six villages.

Valladolid, called Braba,[4] one village.

Chia,[5] one village.

In all, there are sixty-six villages. Tiguex appears to be in the center of the villages. Valladolid is the farthest up the river toward the northeast. The four villages down the river are toward the southeast, because the river turns toward the east.[6] It is 130 leagues—10 more or less—from the farthest point that was seen down the river to the farthest point up the river, and all the settlements are within this region. Including those at a distance, there are sixty-six villages in all, as I have said, and in all of them there may be some 20,000 men, which

Chia), and Cochiti. Acoma and Laguna, to the westward, belong to the same linguistic group. Laguna, however, is a modern pueblo.

[1] One of these was the Tano pueblo of Galisteo, as noted on page 523.

[2] The Jemes pueblo clusters in San Diego and Guadaloupe canyons. See pl. LXX.

[3] The Tewa pueblo of Yugeuingge, where the village of Chamita, above Santa Fé, now stands.

[4] Taos.

[5] The Keres or Queres pueblo of Sia.

[6] The trend of the river in the section of the old pueblo settlements is really westward.

may be taken to be a fair estimate of the
population of the villages. There are no
houses or other buildings between one village and another, but where we went it is
entirely uninhabited. These people, since
they are few, and their manners, government, and habits are so different from all the
nations that have been seen and discovered
in these western regions, must come from
that part of Greater India, the coast of which
lies to the west of this country, for they
could have come down from that country,
crossing the mountain chains and following
down the river, settling in what seemed to
them the best place.[1]   As they multiplied,
they kept on making settlements until they
lost the river when it buried itself underground, its course being in the direction of
Florida.   It comes down from the northeast,
where they [2] could certainly have found signs
of villages.   He preferred, however, to follow
the reports of the Turk, but it would have
been better to cross the mountains where
this river rises.   I believe they would have
found traces of riches and would have reached
the lands from which these people started,
which from its location is on the edge of

[1] The Tusayan Indians belong to the same linguistic stock as the Ute, Comanche, Shoshoni, Bannock,
and others.   The original habitat of the main body
of these tribes was in the far north, although certain
clans of the Tusayan people are of southern origin.
See Powell, Indian Linguistic Families, 7th Annual
Report of the Bureau of Ethnology, p. 108.
[2] The Spaniards under Coronado.

Greater India, although the region is neither known nor understood, because from the trend of the coast it appears that the land between Norway and China is very far up. The country from sea to sea is very wide, judging from the location of both coasts, as well as from what Captain Villalobos discovered when he went in search of China by the sea to the west,[1] and from what has been discovered on the North sea concerning the trend of the coast of Florida toward the Bacallaos, up toward Norway.

To return then to the proposition with which I began, I say that the settlements and people already named were all that were seen in a region 70 leagues wide and 130 long, in the settled country along the river Tiguex. In New Spain there are not one but many establishments, containing a larger number of people. Silver metals were found in many of their villages, which they use for glazing and painting their earthenware.

CHAPTER VII

Which treats of the plains that were crossed, of the cows, and of the people who inhabit them.

WE have spoken of the settlements of high houses which are situated in what seems to be the most level and open part of the moun-

[1] See the Carta escrita por Santisteban á Mendoza, which tells nearly everything that is known of the voyage of Villalobos. We can only surmise what Castañeda may have known about it.

tains, since it is 150 leagues across before entering the level country between the two mountain chains which I said were near the North sea and the South sea, which might better be called the Western sea along this coast. This mountain series is the one which is near the South sea.[1] In order to show that the settlements are in the middle of the mountains, I will state that it is 80 leagues from Chichilticalli, where we began to cross this country, to Cibola; from Cibola, which is the first village, to Cicuye, which is the last on the way across, is 70 leagues; it is 30 leagues from Cicuye to where the plains begin. It may be we went across in an indirect or roundabout way, which would make it seem as if there was more country than if it had been crossed in a direct line, and it may be more difficult and rougher. This can not be known certainly, because the mountains change their direction above the bay at the mouth of the Firebrand (Tizon) river.

Now we will speak of the plains. The country is spacious and level, and is more than 400 leagues wide in the part between the two mountain ranges—one, that which Francisco Vazquez Coronado crossed, and the other that which the force under Don Fernando de Soto crossed, near the North sea, entering the country from Florida. No settlements were seen anywhere on these plains.

[1] More than once Castañeda seems to be addressing those about him where he is writing in Culiacan.

In traversing 250 leagues, the other mountain range was not seen, nor a hill nor a hillock which was three times as high as a man. Several lakes were found at intervals; they were round as plates, a stone's throw or more across, some fresh and some salt. The grass grows tall near these lakes; away from them it is very short, a span or less. The country is like a bowl, so that when a man sits down, the horizon surrounds him all around at the distance of a musket shot. There are no groves of trees except at the rivers, which flow at the bottom of some ravines where the trees grow so thick that they were not noticed until one was right on the edge of them. They are of dead earth. There are paths down into these, made by the cows when they go to the water, which is essential throughout these plains.

As I have related in the first part, people follow the cows, hunting them and tanning the skins to take to the settlements in the winter to sell, since they go there to pass the winter, each company going to those which are nearest, some to the settlements at Cicuye, others toward Quivira, and others to the settlements which are situated in the direction of Florida. These people are called Querechos and Teyas. They described some large settlements, and judging from what was seen of these people and from the accounts they gave of other places, there are a good many more of these people than there are of those at the settlements. They have

111

better figures, are better warriors, and are more feared. They travel like the Arabs, with their tents and troops of dogs loaded with poles [1] and having Moorish pack saddles with girths. When the load gets disarranged, the dogs howl, calling some one to fix them right. These people eat raw flesh and drink blood. They do not eat human flesh. They are a kind people and not cruel. They are faithful friends. They are able to make themselves very well understood by means of signs. They dry the flesh in the sun, cutting it thin like a leaf, and when dry they grind it like meal to keep it and make a sort of sea soup of it to eat. A handful thrown into a pot swells up so as to increase very much. They season it with fat, which they always try to secure when they kill a cow. [2] They empty a large gut and fill it with blood, and carry this around the neck to drink when they are thirsty. When they open the belly of a cow, they squeeze out the chewed grass and drink the juice that remains behind, because they say that this contains the essence of the stomach. They cut the hide open at the back and pull it off at the joints, using a flint as large as a finger, tied in a little stick, with as much ease as if working with a good iron tool. They give it an edge with their own teeth. The quickness with which they do this is something worth seeing and noting.

[1] The well known travois of the plains tribes.
[2] Pemmican.

There are very great numbers of wolves
on these plains, which go around with the
cows. They have white skins. The deer
are pied with white. Their skin is loose,
so that when they are killed it can be pulled
off with the hand while warm, coming off
like pigskin. The rabbits, which are very
numerous, are so foolish that those on horseback killed them with their lances. This is
when they are mounted among the cows.
They fly from a person on foot.

CHAPTER VIII

Of Quivira, of where it is and some information
about it.

QUIVIRA is to the west of those ravines, in
the midst of the country, somewhat nearer
the mountains toward the sea, for the country is level as far as Quivira, and there they
began to see some mountain chains. The
country is well settled. Judging from what
was seen on the borders of it, this country is
very similar to that of Spain in the varieties
of vegetation and fruits. There are plums
like those of Castile, grapes, nuts, mulberries, oats, pennyroyal, wild marjoram, and
large quantities of flax, but this does not do
them any good, because they do not know
how to use it.[1] The people are of almost

[1] Mr. Savage, in the Transactions of the Nebraska
Historical Society, vol. i., p. 198, shows how closely
the descriptions of Castañeda, Jaramillo, and the
others on the expedition, harmonize with the flora
and fauna of his State.

the same sort and appearance as the Teyas.
They have villages like those in New Spain.
The houses are round, without a wall, and
they have one story like a loft, under the
roof, where they sleep and keep their belongings. The roofs are of straw. There are
other thickly settled provinces around it containing large numbers of men. A friar
named Juan de Padilla remained in this
province, together with a Spanish-Portuguese
and a negro and a half-blood and some Indians from the province of Capothan, in New
Spain. They killed the friar because he
wanted to go to the province of the Guas,
who were their enemies. The Spaniard escaped by taking flight on a mare, and afterward reached New Spain, coming out by
way of Panuco. The Indians from New
Spain who accompanied the friar were
allowed by the murderers to bury him, and
then they followed the Spaniard and over-
took him. This Spaniard was a Portuguese,
named Campo.

The great river of the Holy Spirit (Espiritu
Santo),[1] which Don Fernando de Soto discovered in the country of Florida, flows
through this country. It passes through a
province called Arache, according to the
reliable accounts which were obtained here.
The sources were not visited, because, according to what they said, it comes from a
very distant country in the mountains of the

[1] The Mississippi and Missouri rivers.

South sea, from the part that sheds its waters onto the plains. It flows across all the level country and breaks through the mountains of the North sea, and comes out where the people with Don Fernando de Soto navigated it. This is more than 300 leagues from where it enters the sea. On account of this, and also because it has large tributaries, it is so mighty when it enters the sea that they lost sight of the land before the water ceased to be fresh.[1]

This country of Quivira was the last that was seen, of which I am able to give any description or information. Now it is proper for me to return and speak of the army, which I left in Tiguex, resting for the winter, so that it would be able to proceed or return in search of these settlements of Quivira, which was not accomplished after all, because it was God's pleasure that these discoveries should remain for other peoples and that we who had been there should content ourselves with saying that we were the first who discovered it and obtained any information concerning it, just as Hercules knew the site where Julius Cæsar was to found Seville or Hispales. May the all-powerful Lord grant that His will be done in everything. It is certain that if this had not been His will Francisco Vazquez would not have returned to New Spain without cause or reason, as he did, and that it would not have been left for

[1] This is probably a reminiscence of Cabeza de Vaca's narrative.

115

those with Don Fernando de Soto to settle such a good country, as they have done, and besides settling it to increase its extent, after obtaining, as they did, information from our army.[1]

[1] Mota Padilla, cap. xxxiii., 4, p. 166, gives his reasons for the failure of the expedition: "It was most likely the chastisement of God that riches were not found on this expedition, because, when this ought to have been the secondary object of the expedition, and the conversion of all those heathen their first aim, they bartered with fate and struggled after the secondary; and thus the misfortune is not so much that all those labors were without fruit, but the worst is that such a number of souls have remained in their blindness."

THIRD PART

WHICH DESCRIBES WHAT HAPPENED TO
FRANCISCO VAZQUEZ CORONADO DURING
THE WINTER, AND HOW HE GAVE UP
THE EXPEDITION AND RETURNED TO NEW
SPAIN.

Laus Deo.

CHAPTER I

Of how Don Pedro de Tovar came from Señora
with some men, and Don Garcia Lopez de Cardenas
started back to New Spain.

AT the end of the first part of this book,
we told how Francisco Vazquez Coronado,
when he got back from Quivira, gave orders
to winter at Tiguex, in order to return, when
the winter was over, with his whole army
to discover all the settlements in those
regions. Don Pedro de Tovar, who had
gone, as we related, to conduct a force from
the city of Saint Jerome (San Hieronimo),
arrived in the meantime with the men whom
he had brought. He had not selected the
rebels and seditious men there, but the most
experienced ones and the best soldiers—men
whom he could trust—wisely considering
that he ought to have good men in order to
go in search of his general in the country of
the Indian called Turk.

117

Although they found the army at Tiguex when they arrived there, this did not please them much, because they had come with great expectations, believing that they would find their general in the rich country of the Indian called Turk. They consoled themselves with the hope of going back there, and lived in anticipation of the pleasure of undertaking this return expedition, which the army would soon make to Quivira. Don Pedro de Tovar brought letters from New Spain, both from the viceroy, Don Antonio de Mendoza, and from individuals. Among these was one from Don Garcia Lopez de Cardenas, which informed him of the death of his brother, the heir, and summoned him to Spain to receive the inheritance. On this account he was given permission, and left Tiguex with several other persons who received permission to go and settle their affairs. There were many others who would have liked to go, but did not, in order not to appear faint-hearted. During this time the general endeavored to pacify several villages in the neighborhood which were not well disposed, and to make peace with the people at Tiguex. He tried also to procure some of the cloth of the country, because the soldiers were almost naked and poorly clothed, full of lice, which they were unable to get rid of or avoid.

The general, Francisco Vazquez Coronado, had been beloved and obeyed by his captains and soldiers as heartily as any of those who have ever started out in the Indies. Necessity knows no law, and the captains who collected the cloth divided it badly, taking the best for themselves and their friends and soldiers, and leaving the rest for the soldiers, and so there began to be some angry murmuring on account of this. Others also complained because they noticed that some favored ones were spared in the work and in the watches and received better portions of what was divided, both of cloth and food. On this account it is thought that they began to say that there was nothing in the country of Quivira which was worth returning for, which was no slight cause of what afterward happened, as will be seen.

CHAPTER II

Of the general's fall, and of how the return to New Spain was ordered.

AFTER the winter was over, the return to Quivira was announced, and the men began to prepare the things needed. Since nothing in this life is at the disposition of men, but all is under the ordination of Almighty God, it was His will that we should not accomplish this, and so it happened that one feast day the general went out on horseback to amuse himself, as usual, riding with the captain Don Rodrigo Maldonado. He was on a powerful horse, and his servants had put on a new girth, which must have been rotten at the time, for it broke during the race and he fell over on the side where Don Rodrigo was, and as his horse passed over him it hit his head with its hoof, which laid him at the point of death, and his recovery was slow and doubtful.

During this time, while he was in his bed, Don Garcia Lopez de Cardenas, who had started to go to New Spain, came back in flight from Suya, because he had found that town deserted and the people and horses and cattle all dead. When he reached Tiguex and learned the sad news that the general was near his end, as already related, they did not dare to tell him until he had recovered, and when he finally got up and learned of it, it affected him so much that he had to go back to bed again. He may have done this in order to bring about what he afterward accomplished, as was believed later.

It was while he was in this condition that he recollected what a scientific friend of his in Salamanca had told him, that he would become a powerful lord in distant lands, and that he would have a fall from which he would never be able to recover. This expectation of death made him desire to return and die where he had a wife and children. As the physician and surgeon who was doctoring him, and also acted as a talebearer, suppressed the murmurings that were going about among the soldiers, he treated secretly and underhandedly with several gentlemen who agreed with him. They set the soldiers to talking about going back to New Spain, in little knots and gatherings, and induced them to hold consultations about it, and had them send papers to the general, signed by all the soldiers, through their ensigns, asking for this. They all entered into it readily, and not much time needed to be spent, since many desired it already. When they asked him, the general acted as if he did not want to do it, but all the gentlemen and captains supported them, giving him their signed opinions, and as some were in this, they could give it at once, and they even persuaded others to do the same.

Thus they made it seem as if they ought to return to New Spain, because they had not found any riches, nor had they discovered any settled country out of which estates could be formed for all the army. When he had obtained their signatures, the return to New Spain was at once announced, and since nothing can ever be concealed, the double dealing began to be understood, and many of the gentlemen found that they had been deceived and had made a mistake. They tried in every way to get their signatures back again from the general, who guarded them so carefully that he did not go out of one room, making his sickness seem very much worse, and putting guards about his person and room, and at night about the floor on which he slept. In spite of all this, they stole his chest, and it is said that they did not find their signatures in it, because he kept them in his mattress; on the other hand, it is said that they did recover them. They asked the general to give them 60 picked men, with whom they would remain and hold the country until the viceroy could send them support, or recall them, or else that the general would leave them the army and pick out 60 men to go back with him. But the soldiers did not want to remain either way, some because they had turned their prow toward New Spain, and others because they saw clearly the trouble that would arise over who should have the command. The gentlemen, I do not know whether because they had sworn fidelity or because they feared that the soldiers would not support them, did what had been decided on, although with an ill-will, and from this time on they did not obey the general as readily as formerly, and they did not show any affection for him. He made much of the soldiers and humored them, with the result that he did what he desired and secured the return of the whole army.

CHAPTER III

Of the rebellion at Suya and the reasons the settlers gave for it.

WE have already stated in the last chapter that Don Garcia Lopez de Cardenas came back from Suya in flight, having found that

country risen in rebellion. He told how
and why that town was deserted, which occurred as I will relate. The entirely worthless fellows were all who had been left in
that town, the mutinous and seditious men,
besides a few who were honored with the
charge of public affairs and who were left to
govern the others. Thus the bad disposi-
tions of the worthless secured the power,
and they held daily meetings and councils
and declared that they had been betrayed and
were not going to be rescued, since the others
had been directed to go through another part
of the country, where there was a more con-
venient route to New Spain, which was not
so because they were still almost on the
direct road. This talk led some of them to
revolt, and they chose one Pedro de Avila as
their captain.

They went back to Culiacan, leaving the
captain, Diego de Alcaraz, sick in the town
of San Hieronimo, with only a small force.
He did not have anyone whom he could
send after them to compel them to return.
They killed a number of people at several
villages along the way. Finally they reached
Culiacan, where Hernando Arias de Saabedra,
who was waiting for Juan Gallego to come
back from New Spain with a force, detained
them by means of promises, so that Gallego
could take them back. Some who feared
what might happen to them ran away one
night to New Spain. Diego de Alcaraz,
who had remained at Suya with a small

force, sick, was not able to hold his position, although he would have liked to, on account of the poisonous herb which the natives use. When these noticed how weak the Spaniards were, they did not continue to trade with them as they formerly had done. Veins of gold had already been discovered before this, but they were unable to work these, because the country was at war. The disturbance was so great that they did not cease to keep watch and to be more than usually careful.

The town was situated on a little river. One night all of a sudden they saw fires which they were not accustomed to, and on this account they doubled the watches, but not having noticed anything during the whole night, they grew careless along toward morning, and the enemy entered the village so silently that they were not seen until they began to kill and plunder. A number of men reached the plain as well as they could, but while they were getting out the captain was mortally wounded. Several Spaniards came back on some horses after they had recovered themselves and attacked the enemy, rescuing some, though only a few. The enemy went off with the booty, leaving three Spaniards killed, besides many of the servants and more than twenty horses.

The Spaniards who survived started off the same day on foot, not having any horses. They went toward Culiacan, keeping away from the roads, and did not find any food until they reached Corazones, where the Indians, like the good friends they have always been, provided them with food. From here they continued to Culiacan, undergoing great hardships. Hernandarias de Saabedra, the mayor, received them and entertained them as well as he could until Juan Gallego arrived with the reinforcements which he was conducting, on his way to find the army. He was not a little troubled at finding that post deserted, when he expected that the army would be in the rich country which had been described by the Indian called Turk, because he looked like one.

CHAPTER IV

Of how Friar Juan de Padilla and Friar Luis remained in the country and the army prepared to return to Mexico.

WHEN the general, Francisco Vazquez, saw that everything was now quiet, and that his schemes had gone as he wished, he ordered that everything should be ready to start on the return to New Spain by the beginning of the month of April, in the year 1543.[1]

Seeing this, Friar Juan de Padilla, a regular brother of the lesser order,[2] and another, Friar Luis, a lay brother, told the general that they wanted to remain in that country

[1] The correct date is, of course, 1542.
[2] A Franciscan. He was a "frayle de misa."

—Friar Juan de Padilla in Quivira, because his teachings seemed to promise fruit there, and Friar Luis at Cicuye. On this account, as it was Lent at the time, the father made this the subject of his sermon to the companies one Sunday, establishing his proposition on the authority of the Holy Scriptures. He declared his zeal for the conversion of these peoples and his desire to draw them to the faith, and stated that he had received permission to do it, although this was not necessary. The general sent a company to escort them as far as Cicuye, where Friar Luis stopped, while Friar Juan went on back to Quivira with the guides who had conducted the general, taking with him the Portuguese, as we related, and the half-blood, and the Indians from New Spain. He was martyred a short time after he arrived there, as we related in the second part, chapter 8. Thus we may be sure that he died a martyr, because his zeal was holy and earnest.

Friar Luis remained at Cicuye. Nothing more has been heard about him since, but before the army left Tiguex some men who went to take him a number of sheep that were left for him to keep, met him as he was on his way to visit some other villages, which were 15 or 20 leagues from Cicuye, accompanied by some followers. He felt very hopeful that he was liked at the village and that his teaching would bear fruit, although he complained that the old men were falling away from him. I, for my part, believe

that as he was a man of good and holy life,
Our Lord will protect him and give him
grace to convert many of those peoples, and
end his days in guiding them in the faith.
We do not need to believe otherwise, for
the people in those parts are pious and not
at all cruel. They are friends, or rather,
enemies of cruelty, and they remain faithful
and loyal friends.[1]

[1] Gen. W. W. H. Davis, in his Spanish Conquest
of New Mexico, p. 231, gives the following extract,
translated from an old Spanish MS. at Santa Fé:
" When Coronado returned to Mexico, he left behind
him, among the Indians of Cibola, the father fray
Francisco Juan de Padilla, the father fray Juan de
la Cruz, and a Portuguese named Andres del Campo. Soon after the Spaniards departed, Padilla and
the Portuguese set off in search of the country of the
Grand Quivira, where the former understood there
were innumerable souls to be saved. After travel-
ling several days, they reached a large settlement in
the Quivira country. The Indians came out to receive them in battle array, when the friar, knowing
their intentions, told the Portuguese and his attendants to take to flight, while he would await their
coming, in order that they might vent their fury on
him as they ran. The former took to flight, and,
placing themselves on a height within view, saw
what happened to the friar. Padilla awaited their
coming upon his knees, and when they arrived
where he was they immediately put him to death.
The same happened to Juan de la Cruz, who was
left behind at Cibola, which people killed him.
The Portuguese and his attendants made their escape, and ultimately arrived safely in Mexico, where
he told what had occurred." In reply to a request
for further information regarding this manuscript,
General Davis stated that when he revisited Santa
Fé, a few years ago, he learned that one of his suc-
cessors in the post of governor of the territory, having despaired of disposing of the immense mass of
old documents and records deposited in his office,

After the friars had gone, the general, fearing that they might be injured if people were carried away from that country to New Spain, ordered the soldiers to let any of the natives who were held as servants go free to their villages whenever they might wish. In my opinion, though I am not sure, it would have been better if they had been kept and taught among Christians.

The general was very happy and contented when the time arrived and everything needed for the journey was ready, and the army started from Tiguex on its way back to Cibola. One thing of no small note happened during this part of the trip. The horses were in good condition for their work when they started, fat and sleek, but more than thirty died during the ten days which it took to reach Cibola, and there was not a day in which two or three or more did not die. A large number of them also died

by the slow process of using them to kindle fires, had sold the entire lot—an invaluable collection of material bearing on the history of the southwest and its early European and native inhabitants—as junk.

When the reports of these martyrdoms reached New Spain, a number of Franciscans were fired with the zeal of entering the country and carrying on the work thus begun. Several received official permission, and went to the pueblo country. One of them was killed at Tiguex, where most of them settled. A few went on to Cicuye or Pecos, where they found a cross which Padilla had set up. Proceeding to Quivira, the natives there counselled them not to proceed farther. The Indians gave them an account of the death of Fray Padilla, and said that if he had taken their advice he would not have been killed.

afterward before reaching Culiacan, a thing that did not happen during all the rest of the journey.

After the army reached Cibola, it rested before starting across the wilderness, because this was the last of the settlements in that country. The whole country was left well disposed and at peace, and several of our Indian allies remained there.

CHAPTER V

Of how the army left the settlements and marched to Culiacan, and of what happened on the way.

LEAVING astern, as we might say, the settlements that had been discovered in the new land, of which, as I have said, the seven villages of Cibola were the first to be seen and the last that were left, the army started off, marching across the wilderness. The natives kept following the rear of the army for two or three days, to pick up any baggage or servants, for although they were still at peace and had always been loyal friends, when they saw that we were going to leave the country entirely, they were glad to get some of our people in their power, although I do not think that they wanted to injure them, from what I was told by some who were not willing to go back with them when they teased and asked them to. Altogether, they carried off several people besides those who had remained of their own accord, among whom good interpreters could be found today.

The wilderness was crossed without opposition, and on the second day before reaching Chichilticalli Juan Gallego met the army, as he was coming from New Spain with reenforcements of men and necessary supplies for the army, expecting that he would find the army in the country of the Indian called Turk. When Juan Gallego saw that the army was returning, the first thing he said was not, "I am glad you are coming back," and he did not like it any better after he had talked with the general. After he had reached the army, or rather the quarters, there was quite a little movement among the gentlemen toward going back with the new force which had made no slight exertions in coming thus far, having encounters every day with the Indians of these regions who had risen in revolt, as will be related. There was talk of making a settlement somewhere in that region until the viceroy could receive an account of what had occurred. Those soldiers who had come from the new lands would not agree to anything except the return to New Spain, so that nothing came of the proposals made at the consultations, and although there was some opposition, they were finally quieted. Several of the mutineers who had deserted the town of Corazones came with Juan Gallego, who had given them his word as surety for their safety, and even if the general had wanted to punish them, his power was slight, for he had been disobeyed already and was not much respected. He began to be afraid again after this, and made himself sick, and kept a guard.

In several places yells were heard and Indians seen, and some of the horses were wounded and killed, before Batuco[1] was reached, where the friendly Indians from Corazones came to meet the army and see the general. They were always friendly and had treated all the Spaniards who passed through their country well, furnishing them with what food they needed, and men, if they needed these. Our men had always treated them well and repaid them for these things. During this journey the juice of the quince was proved to be a good protection against the poison of the natives, because at one place, several days before reaching Señora, the hostile Indians wounded a Spaniard called Mesa, and he did not die, although the wound of the fresh poison is fatal, and there was a delay of over two hours before curing him with the juice. The poison, however, had left its mark upon him. The skin rotted and fell off until it left the bones and sinews bare, with a horrible smell. The wound was in the wrist,

[1] There were two settlements in Sonora bearing this name, one occupied by the Eudeve and the other by the Tegui division of the Opata. The former village is the one referred to by Castañeda.

and the poison had reached as far as the shoulder when he was cured. The skin on all this fell off.

The army proceeded without taking any rest, because the provisions had begun to fail by this time. These districts were in rebellion, and so there were not any victuals where the soldiers could get them until they reached Petlatlan, although they made several forays into the cross country in search of provisions. Petlatlan is in the province of Culiacan, and on this account was at peace, although they had several surprises after this. The army rested here several days to get provisions. After leaving here they were able to travel more quickly than before, for the 30 leagues of the valley of Culiacan, where they were welcomed back again as people who came with their governor, who had suffered ill treatment.

CHAPTER VI

Of how the general started from Culiacan to give the viceroy an account of the army with which he had been intrusted.

IT seemed, indeed, as if the arrival in the valley of Culiacan had ended the labors of this journey, partly because the general was governor there and partly because it was inhabited by Christians. On this account some began to disregard their superiors and the authority which their captains had over them, and some captains even forgot the obedience due to their general. Each one played his own game, so that while the general was marching toward the town, which was still 10 leagues away, many of the men, or most of them, left him in order to rest in the valley, and some even proposed not to follow him. The general understood that he was not strong enough to compel them, although his position as governor gave him fresh authority. He determined to accomplish it by a better method, which was to order all the captains to provide food and meat from the stores of several villages that were under his control as governor. He pretended to be sick, keeping his bed, so that those who had any business with him could speak to him or he with them more freely, without hindrance or observation, and he kept sending for his particular friends in order to ask them to be sure to speak to the soldiers and encourage them to accompany him back to New Spain, and to tell them that he would request the viceroy, Don Antonio de Mendoza, to show them especial favor, and that he would do so himself for those who might wish to remain in his government. After this had been done, he started with his army at a very bad time, when the rains were beginning, for it was about Saint John's day, at which season it rains continuously.

In the uninhabited country which they passed through as far as Compostela there

are numerous very dangerous rivers, full of
large and fierce alligators. While the army
was halting at one of these rivers, a soldier
who was crossing from one side to the other
was seized, in sight of everybody, and carried off by an alligator without it being possible to help him. The general proceeded,
leaving the men who did not want to follow
him all along the way, and reached Mexico
with less than 100 men. He made his report to the viceroy, Don Antonio de Mendoza, who did not receive him very gra-
ciously, although he gave him his discharge.
His reputation was gone from this time on.
He kept the government of New Galicia,
which had been entrusted to him, for only a
short time, when the viceroy took it himself,
until the arrival of the court, or audiencia,
which still governs it. And this was the
end of those discoveries and of the expedition which was made to these new lands.

It now remains for us to describe the way
in which to enter the country by a more
direct route, although there is never a short
cut without hard work. It is always best
to find out what those know who have prepared the way, who know what will be
needed. This can be found elsewhere, and
I will now tell where Quivira lies, what direction the army took, and the direction in
which Greater India lies, which was what
they pretended to be in search of, when the
army started thither. Today, since Villalobos has discovered that this part of the coast

of the South sea trends toward the west, it
is clearly seen and acknowledged that, since
we were in the north, we ought to have
turned to the west instead of toward the
east, as we did. With this, we will leave
this subject and will proceed to finish this
treatise, since there are several noteworthy
things of which I must give an account,
which I have left to be treated more extensively in the two following chapters.

CHAPTER VII

Of the adventures of Captain Juan Gallego while
he was bringing reenforcements through the revolted
country.

ONE might well have complained when
in the last chapter I passed in silence over
the exploits of Captain Juan Gallego with
his 20 companions. I will relate them in
the present chapter, so that in times to come
those who read about it or tell of it may
have a reliable authority on whom to rely.
I am not writing fables, like some of the
things which we read about nowadays in the
books of chivalry. If it were not that those
stories contained enchantments, there are
some things which our Spaniards have done
in our own day in these parts, in their conquests and encounters with the Indians,
which, for deeds worthy of admiration, sur-
pass not only the books already mentioned,
but also those which have been written

about the twelve peers of France, because, if the deadly strength which the authors of those times attributed to their heroes and the brilliant and resplendent arms with which they adorned them, are fully considered, and compared with the small stature of the men of our time and the few and poor weapons which they have in these parts,[1] the remarkable things which our people have undertaken and accomplished with such weapons are more to be wondered at today than those of which the ancients write, and just because, too, they fought with barbarous naked people, as ours have with Indians, among whom there are always men who are brave and valiant and very sure bowmen, for we have seen them pierce the wings while flying, and hit hares while running after them. I have said all this in order to show that some things which we consider fables may be true, because we see greater things every day in our own times, just as in future times people will greatly wonder at the deeds of Don Fernando Cortez, who dared to go into the midst of New Spain with 300 men against the vast number of people in Mexico, and who with 500 Spaniards succeeded in subduing it, and made himself lord over it in two years.

The deeds of Don Pedro de Alvarado in

---

[1] The letters of Mendoza during the early part of his administration in Mexico repeatedly call attention to the lack of arms and ammunition among the Spaniards in the New World.

the conquest of Guatemala, and those of Montejo in Tabasco, the conquests of the mainland and of Peru, were all such as to make me remain silent concerning what I now wish to relate; but since I have promised to give an account of what happened on this journey, I want the things I am now going to relate to be known as well as those others of which I have spoken.

The captain Juan Gallego, then, reached the town of Culiacan with a very small force. There he collected as many as he could of those who had escaped from the town of Hearts, or, more correctly, from Suya, which made in all 22 men, and with these he marched through all of the settled country, across which he traveled 200 leagues with the country in a state of war and the people in rebellion, although they had formerly been friendly toward the Spaniards, having encounters with the enemy almost every day. He always marched with the advance guard, leaving two-thirds of his force behind with the baggage. With six or seven Spaniards, and without any of the Indian allies whom he had with him, he forced his way into their villages, killing and destroying and setting them on fire, coming upon the enemy so suddenly and with such quickness and boldness that they did not have a chance to collect or even to do anything at all, until they became so afraid of him that there was not a town which dared wait for him, but they fled before him as from a powerful army; so much so, that for ten days, while he was passing through the settlements, they did not have an hour's rest.

He did all this with his seven companions, so that when the rest of the force came up with the baggage there was nothing for them to do except to pillage, since the others had already killed and captured all the people they could lay their hands on and the rest had fled. They did not pause anywhere, so that although the villages ahead of him received some warning, they were upon them so quickly that they did not have a chance to collect. Especially in the region where the town of Hearts had been, he killed and hung a large number of people to punish them for their rebellion. He did not lose a companion during all this, nor was anyone wounded, except one soldier, who was wounded in the eyelid by an Indian who was almost dead, whom he was stripping. The weapon broke the skin and, as it was poisoned, he would have had to die if he had not been saved by the quince juice; he lost his eye as it was.

These deeds of theirs were such that I know those people will remember them as long as they live, and especially four or five friendly Indians who went with them from Corazones, who thought that they were so wonderful that they held them to be something divine rather than human. If he had not fallen in with our army as he did, they would have reached the country of the In-

dian called Turk, which they expected to
march to, and they would have arrived there
without danger on account of their good
order and the skill with which he was leading them, and their knowledge and ample
practice in war. Several of these men are
still in this town of Culiacan, where I am
now writing this account and narrative,
where they, as well as I and the others who
have remained in this province, have never
lacked for labor in keeping this country
quiet, in capturing rebels, and increasing in
poverty and need, and more than ever at the
present hour, because the country is poorer
and more in debt than ever before.

CHAPTER VIII

Which describes some remarkable things that were
seen on the plains, with a description of the bulls.

My silence was not without mystery and
dissimulation when, in chapter 7 of the
second part of this book, I spoke of the
plains and of the things of which I will give
a detailed account in this chapter, where all
these things may be found together; for
these things were remarkable and something
not seen in other parts. I dare to write of
them because I am writing at a time when
many men are still living who saw them
and who will vouch for my account. Who
could believe that 1,000 horses and 500 of
our cows and more than 5,000 rams and

ewes and more than 1,500 friendly Indians and servants, in traveling over those plains, would leave no more trace where they had passed than if nothing had been there— nothing—so that it was necessary to make piles of bones and cow dung now and then, so that the rear guard could follow the army. The grass never failed to become erect after it had been trodden down, and, although it was short, it was as fresh and straight as before.

Another thing was a heap of cow bones, a crossbow shot long, or a very little less, almost twice a man's height in places, and some 18 feet or more wide, which was found on the edge of a salt lake in the southern part, and this in a region where there are no people who could have made it. The only explanation of this which could be suggested was that the waves which the north winds must make in the lake had piled up the bones of the cattle which had died in the lake, when the old and weak ones who went into the water were unable to get out. The noticeable thing is the number of cattle that would be necessary to make such a pile of bones.

Now that I wish to describe the appearance of the bulls, it is to be noticed first that there was not one of the horses that did not take flight when he saw them first, for they have a narrow, short face, the brow two palms across from eye to eye, the eyes sticking out at the side, so that, when they are running, they can see who is following them. They have very long beards, like goats, and when they are running they throw their heads back with the beard dragging on the ground. There is a sort of girdle round the middle of the body. The hair is very woolly, like a sheep's, very fine, and in front of the girdle the hair is very long and rough like a lion's. They have a great hump, larger than a camel's. The horns are short and thick, so that they are not seen much above the hair. In May they change the hair in the middle of the body for a down, which makes perfect lions of them. They rub against the small trees in the little ravines to shed their hair, and they continue this until only the down is left, as a snake changes his skin. They have a short tail, with a bunch of hair at the end. When they run, they carry it erect like a scorpion. It is worth noticing that the little calves are red and just like ours, but they change their color and appearance with time and age.

Another strange thing was that all the bulls that were killed had their left ears slit, although these were whole when young. The reason for this was a puzzle that could not be guessed. The wool ought to make good cloth on account of its fineness, although the color is not good, because it is the color of buriel.[1]

[1] The kersey, or coarse woollen cloth out of which the habits of the Franciscan friars were made. Hence the name, grey friars.

Another thing worth noticing is that the bulls traveled without cows in such large numbers that nobody could have counted them, and so far away from the cows that it was more than 40 leagues from where we began to see the bulls to the place where we began to see the cows. The country they traveled over was so level and smooth that if one looked at them the sky could be seen between their legs, so that if some of them were at a distance they looked like smooth-trunked pines whose tops joined, and if there was only one bull it looked as if there were four pines. When one was near them, it was impossible to see the ground on the other side of them. The reason for all this was that the country seemed as round as if a man should imagine himself in a three-pint measure, and could see the sky at the edge of it, about a crossbow shot from him, and even if a man only lay down on his back he lost sight of the ground.[1]

I have not written about other things which were seen nor made any mention of them, because they were not of so much importance, although it does not seem right for me to remain silent concerning the fact that they venerate the sign of the cross in the region where the settlements have high houses. For at a spring which was in the plain near Acuco they had a cross two palms

[1] The earliest description of the American buffalo by a European is in Cabeza de Vaca's Naufragios, fol. xxvii., verso (ed. 1555).

high and as thick as a finger, made of wood
with a square twig for its crosspiece, and
many little sticks decorated with feathers
around it, and numerous withered flowers,
which were the offerings.[1] In a graveyard
outside the village at Tutahaco there appeared to have been a recent burial. Near
the head there was another cross made of
two little sticks tied with cotton thread, and
dry withered flowers. It certainly seems to
me that in some way they must have received some light from the cross of Our
Redeemer, Christ, and it may have come by
way of India, from whence they proceeded.

CHAPTER IX

Which treats of the direction which the army
took, and of how another more direct way might be
found, if anyone was to return to that country.

I VERY much wish that I possessed some
knowledge of cosmography or geography, so
as to render what I wish to say intelligible,
and so that I could reckon up or measure
the advantage those people who might go in
search of that country would have if they
went directly through the center of the

[1] Scattered through the papers of Dr. J. Walter
Fewkes on the Zuñi and Tusayan Indians will be
found many descriptions of the páhos or prayer
sticks and other forms used as offerings at the
shrines, together with exact accounts of the manner
of making the offerings.

country, instead of following the road the army took. However, with the help of the favor of the Lord, I will state it as well as I can, making it as plain as possible.

It is, I think, already understood that the Portuguese, Campo, was the soldier who escaped when Friar Juan de Padilla was killed at Quivira, and that he finally reached New Spain from Panuco,[1] having traveled across the plains country until he came to cross the North Sea mountain chain, keeping the country that Don Hernando de Soto discovered all the time on his left hand, since he did not see the river of the Holy Spirit (Espiritu Santo) at all.[2] After he had crossed the North Sea mountains, he found that he was in Panuco, so that if he had not tried to go to the North sea, he would have come out in the neighborhood of the border

[1] The northeastern province of New Spain.
[2] The conception of the great inland plain stretching between the great lakes at the head of the St. Lawrence and the Gulf of Mexico came to cosmographers very slowly. Almost all of the early maps show a disposition to carry the mountains which follow the Atlantic coast along the gulf coast as far as Texas, a result, doubtless, of the fact that all the expeditions which started inland from Florida found mountains. Coronado's journey to Quivira added but little to the detailed geographical knowledge of America. The name reached Europe, and it is found on the maps, along the fortieth parallel, almost everywhere from the Pacific coast to the neighborhood of a western tributary to the St. Lawrence system. See the maps reproduced herein. Castañeda could have aided them considerably, but the map makers did not know of his book.

land, or the country of the Sacatecas,[1] of which we now have some knowledge.

This way would be somewhat better and more direct for anyone going back there in search of Quivira, since some of those who came with the Portuguese are still in New Spain to serve as guides. Nevertheless, I think it would be best to go through the country of the Guachichules, keeping near the South Sea mountains all the time, for there are more settlements and a food supply, for it would be suicide to launch out on to the plains country, because it is so vast and is barren of anything to eat, although, it is true, there would not be much need of this after coming to the cows.

This is only when one goes in search of Quivira, and of the villages which were described by the Indian called Turk, for the army of Francisco Vazquez Coronado went the very farthest way round to get there, since they started from Mexico and went 110 leagues to the west, and then 100 leagues to the northeast, and 250 to the north, and all this brought them as far as the ravines where the cows were, and after traveling 850 leagues they were not more

[1] Captain John Stevens' Dictionary says that this is " a northern province of North America, rich in silver mines, but ill provided with water, grain, and other substances; yet by reason of the mines there are seven or eight Spanish towns in it." Zacatecas is now one of the central states of the Mexican confederation, being south of Coahuila and southeast of Durango.

than 400 leagues distant from Mexico by a direct route. If one desires to go to the country of Tiguex, so as to turn from there toward the west in search of the country of India, he ought to follow the road taken by the army, for there is no other, even if one wished to go by a different way, because the arm of the sea which reaches into this coast toward the north does not leave room for any. But what might be done is to have a fleet and cross this gulf and disembark in the neighborhood of the Island of Negroes [1] and enter the country from there, crossing the mountain chains in search of the country from which the people at Tiguex came, or other peoples of the same sort.

As for entering from the country of Florida and from the North sea, it has already been observed that the many expeditions which have been undertaken from that side have been unfortunate and not very successful, because that part of the country is full of bogs and poisonous fruits, barren, and the very worst country that is warmed by the sun. But they might disembark after passing the river of the Holy Spirit, as Don Hernando de Soto did. Nevertheless, despite the fact that I underwent much labor, I still think that the way I went to that country

[1] Apparently the location of this island gradually drifted westward with the increase of geographical knowledge, until it was finally located in the Philippine group.

is the best.   There ought to be river courses, because the necessary supplies can be carried on these more easily in large quantities. Horses are the most necessary things in the new countries, and they frighten the enemy most. . . . Artillery is also much feared by those who do not know how to use it.   A piece of heavy artillery would be very good for settlements like those which Francisco Vazquez Coronado discovered, in order to knock them down, because he had nothing but some small machines for slinging and nobody skillful enough to make a catapult or some other machine which would frighten them, which is very necessary.

I say, then, that with what we now know about the trend of the coast of the South sea, which has been followed by the ships which explored the western part, and what is known of the North sea toward Norway, the coast of which extends up from Florida, those who now go to discover the country which Francisco Vazquez entered, and reach the country of Cibola or of Tiguex, will know the direction in which they ought to go in order to discover the true direction of the country which the Marquis of the Valley, Don Hernando Cortes, tried to find, following the direction of the gulf of the Firebrand (Tizon) river.   This will suffice for the conclusion of our narrative.   Everything else rests on the powerful Lord of all things, God Omnipotent, who knows how and when these lands will be discovered and

147

for whom He has guarded this good fortune.

Laus Deo.

Finished copying, Saturday the 26th of October, 1596, in Seville.

TRANSLATION OF THE LETTER FROM MENDOZA TO THE KING, APRIL 17, 1540.[1]

S. C. C. M.:

I wrote to Your Majesty from Compostela the last of February, giving you an account of my arrival there and of the departure of Francisco Vazquez with the force which I sent to pacify and settle in the newly discovered country, and of how the warden, Lope de Samaniego, was going as army master, both because he was a responsible person and a very good Christian, and because he has had experience in matters of this sort; as Your Majesty had desired to know. And the news which I have received since then is to the effect that after they had passed the uninhabited region of Culuacan and were approaching Chiametla, the warden went off with some horsemen to find provisions, and one of the soldiers who was with him, who had strayed from the force, called out that they were killing him. The warden hastened to his assistance, and they wounded him in the eye with an arrow, from which

[1] From the Spanish text in Pacheco y Cardenas, Documentos de Indias, vol. ii., p. 356. The letter mentioned in the opening sentence is not known to exist.

he died. In regard to the fortress,[1] besides the fact that it is badly built and going to pieces, it seems to me that the cost of it is excessive, and that Your Majesty could do without the most of it, because there is one man who takes charge of the munitions and artillery, and an armorer to repair it, and a gunner, and as this is the way it was under the audiencia, before the fortresses were made conformable to what I have written to Your Majesty, we can get along without the rest, because that fortress was built on account of the brigantines, and not for any other purpose.[2] And as the lagoon is so dry that it can do no good in this way for the present, I think that, for this reason, the cost is superfluous. I believe that it will have fallen in before a reply can come from Your Majesty.

Some days ago I wrote to Your Majesty that I had ordered Melchior Diaz, who was in the town of San Miguel de Culuacan, to take some horsemen and see if the account given by the father, Friar Marcos, agreed with what he could discover. He set out from Culuacan with fifteen horsemen, the 17th of November last. The 20th of this present March I received a letter from him, which he sent me by Juan de Zaldyvar and

---

[1] Presumably the fortress of which Samaniego was warden.
[2] Buckingham Smith's Florida gives many documents relating to the damage done by French brigantines to the Spanish West Indies during 1540–41.

three other horsemen. In this he says that
after he left Culuacan and crossed the river
of Petatlan he was everywhere very well received by the Indians. The way he did was
to send a cross to the place where he was
going to stop, because this was a sign which
the Indians received with deep veneration,
making a house out of mats in which to place
it, and somewhat away from this they made
a lodging for the Spaniards, and drove stakes
where they could tie the horses, and supplied
fodder for them, and abundance of corn
wherever they had it. They say that they
suffered from hunger in many places, because
it had been a bad year. After going 100
leagues from Culuacan, he began to find the
country cold, with severe frosts, and the
farther he went on the colder it became, until
he reached a point where some Indians whom
he had with him were frozen, and two Spaniards were in great danger. Seeing this, he
decided not to go any farther until the winter was over, and to send back, by those whom
I mentioned, an account of what he had
learned concerning Cibola and the country
beyond, which is as follows, taken literally
from his letter:

"I have given Your Lordship an account
of what happened to me along the way; and
seeing that it is impossible to cross the uninhabited region which stretches from here
to Cibola, on account of the heavy snows
and the cold, I will give Your Lordship an
account of what I have learned about Cibola,

which I have ascertained by asking many persons who have been there fifteen and twenty years; and I have secured this in many different ways, taking some Indians together and others separately, and on comparison they all seem to agree in what they say. After crossing this large wilderness, there are seven places, being a short day's march from one to another, all of which are together called Cibola. The houses are of stone and mud, coarsely worked. They are made in this way: One large wall, and at each end of this wall some rooms are built, partitioned off 20 feet square, according to the description they give, which are planked with square beams. Most of the houses are reached from the flat roofs, using their ladders to go to the streets. The houses have three and four stories. They declare that there are few having two stories. The stories are mostly half as high again as a man, except the first one, which is low, and only a little more than a man's height. One ladder is used to communicate with ten or twelve houses together. They make use of the low ones and live in the highest ones. In the lowest ones of all they have some loopholes made sideways, as in the fortresses of Spain. The Indians say that when these people are attacked, they station themselves in their houses and fight from there; and that when they go to make war, they carry shields and wear leather jackets, which are made of cows' hide, colored, and that they fight with arrows and with a sort of stone maul and with some other weapons made of sticks, which I have not been able to make out. They eat human flesh, and they keep those whom they capture in war as slaves. There are many fowls in the country, tame. They have much corn and beans and melons [squashes]. In their houses they keep some hairy animals, like the large Spanish hounds, which they shear, and they make long colored wigs from the hair, like this one which I send to Your Lordship, which they wear, and they also put this same stuff in the cloth which they make.[1] The men are of small stature [plate LXII]; the women are light colored and of good appearance, and they wear shirts or chemises which reach down to their feet. They wear their hair on each side done up in a sort of twist [plate LXIII], which leaves the ears outside, in which they hang many turquoises, as well as on their necks and on the wrists of their arms. The clothing of the men is a cloak, and over this the skin of a cow, like the one which Cabeza de Vaca and Dorantes brought, which Your Lordship saw; they wear caps[2] on their heads; in summer they wear shoes made of

[1] In his paper on the Human Bones of the Hemenway Collection (Memoirs of the National Academy of Sciences, VI., p. 156 et seq.), Dr. Washington Matthews discusses the possible former existence of a variety of the llama in certain parts of the southwest.

[2] The headbands are doubtless here referred to.

painted or colored skin, and high buskins in winter.

"They were also unable to tell me of any metal, nor did they say that they had it. They have turquoises in quantity, although not so many as the father provincial said. They have some little stone crystals, like this which I send to Your Lordship, of which Your Lordship has seen many here in New Spain. They cultivate the ground in the same way as in New Spain. They carry things on their heads, as in Mexico. The men weave cloth and spin cotton. They have salt from a marshy lake, which is two days from the province of Cibola.[1] The Indians have their dances and songs, with some flutes which have holes on which to put the fingers. They make much noise. They sing in unison with those who play, and those who sing clap their hands in our fashion. One of the Indians that accompanied the negro Esteban, who had been a captive there, saw the playing as they practiced it, and others singing as I have said, although not very vigorously. They say that five or six play together, and that some of the flutes are better than others.[2] They say the country is good for corn and beans, and that they do not have any fruit trees,

[1] The same salt lake from which the Zuñis obtain their salt supply to-day.

[2] Compare with this hearsay description of something almost unknown to the Spaniards, the thoroughly scientific descriptions of the Hopi dances and ceremonials recorded by Dr. J. Walter Fewkes.

nor do they know what such a thing is.[1]
They have very good mountains. The
country lacks water. They do not raise cotton, but bring it from Totonteac.[2] They eat
out of flat bowls, like the Mexicans. They
raise considerable corn and beans and other
similar things. They do not know what sea
fish is, nor have they ever heard of it. I
have not obtained any information about the
cows, except that these are found beyond the
province of Cibola. There is a great abundance of wild goats, of the color of bay horses;
there are many of these here where I am,
and although I have asked the Indians if
those are like these, they tell me no. Of
the seven settlements, they describe three of
them as very large; four not so big. They
describe them, as I understand, to be about
three crossbow shots square for each place,
and from what the Indians say, and their
descriptions of the houses and their size, and

[1] The peaches, watermelons, cantaloupes, and
grapes, now so extensively cultivated by the Pueblos, were introduced early in the seventeenth cen-
tury by the Spanish missionaries.

[2] At first glance it seems somewhat strange that
although Zuñi is considerably more than 100 miles
south of Totonteac, or Tusayan, the people of the
former villages did not cultivate cotton, but in this
I am reminded by Mr. Hodge that part of the Tusayan people are undoubtedly of southern origin
and that in all probability they introduced cotton
into that group of villages. The Pimas raised
cotton as late as 1850. None of the Pueblos now
cultivate the plant, the introduction of cheap fab-
rics by traders having doubtless brought the indus-
try to an end.

as these are close together, and considering that there are people in each house, it ought to make a large multitude. Totonteac is declared to be seven short days from the province of Cibola, and of the same sort of houses and people, and they say that cotton grows there. I doubt this, because they tell me that it is a cold country. They say that there are twelve villages, every one of which is larger than the largest at Cibola. They also tell me that there is a village which is one day from Cibola, and that the two are at war.[1] They have the same sort of houses and people and customs. They declare this to be greater than any of those described; I take it that there is a great multitude of people there. They are very well known, on account of having these houses and abundance of food and turquoises. I have not been able to learn more than what I have related, although, as I have said, I have had with me Indians who have lived there fifteen and twenty years.

"The death of Esteban the negro took place in the way the father, Friar Marcos, described it to your lordship, and so I do not make a report of it here, except that the people at Cibola sent word to those of this village and in its neighborhood that if any

---

[1] Doubtless the pueblo of Marata (Makyata) mentioned by Marcos de Niza. This village was situated near the salt lake and had been destroyed by the Zuñis some years before Niza visited New Mexico.

Christians should come, they ought not to consider them as anything peculiar, and ought to kill them, because they were mortal —saying that they had learned this because they kept the bones of the one who had come there; and that, if they did not dare to do this, they should send word so that those (at Cibola) could come and do it. I can very easily believe that all this has taken place, and that there has been some communication between these places, because of the coolness with which they received us and the sour faces they have shown us."

Melchior Diaz says that the people whom he found along the way do not have any settlements at all, except in one valley which is 150 leagues from Culuacan, which is well settled and has houses with lofts, and that there are many people along the way, but that they are not good for anything except to make them Christians, as if this was of small account. May Your Majesty remember to provide for the service of God, and keep in mind the deaths and the loss of life and of provinces which has taken place in these Indies. And, moreover, up to this present day none of the things Your Majesty has commanded, which have been very holy and good, have been attended to, nor priests provided, either for that country or for this. For I assure Your Majesty that there is no trace of Christianity where they have not yet arrived, neither little nor much, and that the poor people are ready to receive the priests and come to them even when they flee from us like deer in the mountains. And I state this because I am an eyewitness, and I have seen it clearly during this trip. I have importuned Your Majesty for friars, and yet again I can not cease doing it much more, because unless this be done I can not accomplish that which I am bound to do.

After I reach Mexico, I will give Your Majesty an account of everything concerning these provinces, for while I should like to do it today, I can not, because I am very weak from a slow fever which I caught in Colima, which attacked me very severely, although it did not last more than six days. It has pleased Our Lord to make me well already, and I have traveled here to Jacona, where I am.

May Our Lord protect the Holy Catholic Cæsarian person of Your Majesty and aggrandize it with increase of better kingdoms and lordships, as we your servants desire.

From Jacona, April 17, 1540.

S. C. C. M.

Your Holy Majesty's humble servant, who salutes your royal feet and hands,
D. ANTONIO DE MENDOZA.

TRANSLATION OF THE LETTER FROM CORONADO TO MENDOZA, AUGUST 3, 1540 [1]

THE ACCOUNT GIVEN BY FRANCISCO VAZQUEZ DE CORONADO, CAPTAIN-GENERAL OF THE FORCE WHICH WAS SENT IN THE NAME OF HIS MAJESTY TO THE NEWLY DISCOVERED COUNTRY, OF WHAT HAPPENED TO THE EXPEDITION AFTER APRIL 22 OF THE YEAR MDXL, WHEN HE STARTED FORWARD FROM CULIACAN, AND OF WHAT HE FOUND IN THE COUNTRY THROUGH WHICH HE PASSED.

I

Francisco Vazquez starts from Culiacan with his army, and after suffering various inconveniences on account of the badness of the way, reaches the Valley of Hearts, where he failed to find any corn, to procure which he sends to the valley called Señora. He receives an account of the important Valley of Hearts and of the people there, and of some lands lying along that coast.

ON the 22d of the month of April last, I set out from the province of Culiacan with a part of the army, having made the arrange-

---

[1] Translated from the Italian version, in Ramusio's Viaggi, vol. iii., fol. 359 (ed. 1556). There is another English translation in Hakluyt's Voyages, vol. iii., p. 373 (ed. 1600). Hakluyt's translation is reprinted in Old South Leaflet, general series, No. 20. The proper names, excepting such as are properly translated, are spelled as in the Italian text.

ments of which I wrote to Your Lordship. Judging by the outcome, I feel sure that it was fortunate that I did not start the whole of the army on this undertaking, because the labors have been so very great and the lack of food such that I do not believe this undertaking could have been completed before the end of this year, and that there would be a great loss of life if it should be accomplished. For, as I wrote to Your Lordship, I spent eighty days in traveling to Culiacan,[1] during which time I and the gentlemen of my company, who were horsemen, carried on our backs and on our horses a little food, in such wise that after leaving this place none of us carried any necessary effects weighing more than a pound. For all this, and although we took all possible care and forethought of the small supply of provisions which we carried, it gave out. And this is not to be wondered at, because the road is rough and long, and what with our harquebuses, which had to be carried up the mountains and hills and in the passage of the rivers, the greater part of the corn was lost. And since I send Your Lordship a drawing of this route, I will say no more about it here.

[1] This statement is probably not correct. It may be due to a blunder by Ramusio in translating from the original text. Eighty days would be nearly the time which Coronado probably spent on the journey from Culiacan to Cibola, and this interpretation would render the rest of the sentence much more intelligible.

Thirty leagues before reaching the place which the father provincial spoke so well of in his report,[1] I sent Melchior Diaz forward with fifteen horsemen, ordering him to make but one day's journey out of two, so that he could examine everything there before I arrived. He traveled through some very rough mountains for four days, and did not find anything to live on, nor people, nor information about anything, except that he found two or three poor villages, with twenty or thirty huts apiece. From the people here he learned that there was nothing to be found in the country beyond except the mountains, which continued very rough, entirely uninhabited by people. And, because this was labor lost, I did not want to send Your Lordship an account of it. The whole company felt disturbed at this, that a thing so much praised, and about which the father had said so many things, should be found so very different; and they began to think that all the rest would be of the same sort.

When I noticed this, I tried to encourage them as well as I could, telling them that Your Lordship had always thought that this part of the trip would be a waste of effort, and that we ought to devote our attention to those Seven Cities and the other provinces about which we had information—that these should be the end of our enterprise. With this resolution and purpose, we all marched

[1] The valley into which Friar Marcos did not dare to enter

cheerfully along a very bad way, where it was impossible to pass without making a new road or repairing the one that was there, which troubled the soldiers not a little, considering that everything which the friar had said was found to be quite the reverse; because, among other things which the father had said and declared, he said that the way would be plain and good, and that there would be only one small hill of about half a league. And the truth is, that there are mountains where, however well the path might be fixed, they could not be crossed without there being great danger of the horses falling over them. And it was so bad that a large number of the animals which Your Lordship sent as provision for the army were lost along this part of the way, on account of the roughness of the rocks. The lambs and wethers lost their hoofs along the way, and I left the greater part of those which I brought from Culiacan at the river of Lachimi,[1] because they were unable to travel, and so that they might proceed more slowly.

Four horsemen remained with them, who have just arrived. They have not brought more than 24 lambs and 4 wethers; the rest died from the toil, although they did not travel more than two leagues daily. I reached the Valley of Hearts at last, on the 26th day of the month of May, and rested

---

[1] Doubtless the Yaquimi or Yaqui river.

there a number of days. Between Culiacan
and this place I could sustain myself only
by means of a large supply of corn bread,
because I had to leave all the corn, as it was
not yet ripe. In this Valley of Hearts we
found more people than in any part of the
country which we had left behind, and a
large extent of tilled ground. There was no
corn for food among them, but as I heard
that there was some in another valley called
Señora, which I did not wish to disturb by
force, I sent Melchior Diaz with goods to
exchange for it, so as to give this to the
friendly Indians whom we brought with us,
and to some who had lost their animals
along the way and had not been able to
carry the food which they had taken from
Culiacan. By the favor of Our Lord, some
little corn was obtained by this trading,
which relieved the friendly Indians and
some Spaniards. Ten or twelve of the
horses had died of overwork by the time that
we reached this Valley of Hearts, because
they were unable to stand the strain of carrying heavy burdens and eating little. Some
of our negroes and some of the Indians also
died here, which was not a slight loss for
the rest of the expedition. They told me
that the Valley of Hearts is a long five-days'
journey from the western sea. I sent to
summon Indians from the coast in order to
learn about their condition, and while I was
waiting for these the horses rested. I stayed
there four days, during which the Indians

came from the sea, who told me that there
were seven or eight islands two days' journey
from that seacoast, directly opposite, well
populated with people, but poorly supplied
with food, and the people were savages.[1]
They told me they had seen a ship pass
not very far from the land. I do not know
whether to think that it was the one which
was sent to discover the country, or perhaps
some Portuguese.[2]

II

They come to Chichilticale; after having taken
two days' rest, they enter a country containing very
little food and hard to travel for 30 leagues, beyond
which the country becomes pleasant, and there is a
river called the River of the Flax (del Lino); they
fight against the Indians, being attacked by these;
and having by their victory secured the city, they
relieve themselves of the pangs of their hunger.

I SET out from the Hearts and kept near
the seacoast as well as I could judge, but in
fact I found myself continually farther off,
so that when I reached Chichilticale I found
that I was fifteen days' journey distant from
the sea, although the father provincial had

[1] These were doubtless the Seri, of Yuman stock,
who occupied a strip of the Gulf coast between lati-
tude 28° and 29° and the islands Angel de la Guardia
and Tiburon. The latter island, as well as the
coast of the adjacent mainland, is still inhabited by
this tribe.

[2] As Indian news goes, there is no reason why this
may not have been one of Ulloa's ships, which sailed
along this coast during the previous summer. It
can hardly have been a ship of Alarcon's fleet.

said that it was only 5 leagues distant and that he had seen it. We all became very distrustful, and felt great anxiety and dismay to see that everything was the reverse of what he had told Your Lordship. The Indians of Chichilticale say that when they go to the sea for fish, or for anything else that they need, they go across the country, and that it takes them ten days; and this information which I have received from the Indians appears to me to be true. The sea turns toward the west directly opposite the Hearts for 10 or 12 leagues, where I learned that the ships of Your Lordship had been seen, which had gone in search of the port of Chichilticale, which the father said was on the thirty-fifth degree.

God knows what I have suffered, because I fear that they may have met with some mishap. If they follow the coast, as they said they would, as long as the food lasts which they took with them, of which I left them a supply in Culiacan, and if they have not been overtaken by some misfortune, I maintain my trust in God that they have already discovered something good, for which the delay which they have made may be pardoned. I rested for two days at Chichilticale, and there was good reason for staying longer, because we found that the horses were becoming so tired; but there was no chance to rest longer, because the food was giving out. I entered the borders of the wilderness region on Saint John's eve, and,

for a change from our past labors, we found
no grass during the first days, but a worse
way through mountains and more dangerous
passages than we had experienced previously.
The horses were so tired that they were not
equal to it, so that in this last desert we lost
more horses than before; and some Indian
allies and a Spaniard called Spinosa, besides
two negroes, died from eating some herbs
because the food had given out.

I sent the army-master, Don Garcia Lopez
de Cardenas, with 15 horsemen, a day's
march ahead of me, in order to explore the
country and prepare the way, which he accomplished like the man that he is, and
agreeably to the confidence which Your Lordship has had in him. I am the more certain
that he did so, because, as I have said, the
way is very bad for at least 30 leagues and
more, through impassable mountains. But
when we had passed these 30 leagues, we
found fresh rivers and grass like that of Castile, and especially one sort like what we
call *Scaramoio;* many nut and mulberry
trees, but the leaves of the nut trees are different from those of Spain. There was a
considerable amount of flax near the banks
of one river, which was called on this account El Rio del Lino. No Indians were
seen during the first day's march, after which
four Indians came out with signs of peace,
saying that they had been sent to that
desert place to say that we were welcome,
and that on the next day the tribe would

provide the whole force with food. The army-master gave them a cross, telling them to say to the people in their city that they need not fear, and that they should have their people stay in their own houses, because I was coming in the name of His Majesty to defend and help them.

After this was done, Ferrando Alvarado came back to tell me that some Indians had met him peaceably, and that two of them were with the army-master waiting for me. I went to them forthwith and gave them some paternosters and some little cloaks, telling them to return to their city and say to the people there that they could stay quietly in their houses and that they need not fear. After this I ordered the army-master to go and see if there were any bad passages which the Indians might be able to defend, and to seize and hold any such until the next day, when I would come up. He went, and found a very bad place in our way where we might have received much harm. He immediately established himself there with the force which he was conducting. The Indians came that very night to occupy that place so as to defend it, and finding it taken, they assaulted our men. According to what I have been told, they attacked like valiant men, although in the end they had to retreat in flight, because the army-master was on the watch and kept his men in good order. The Indians sounded a little trumpet as a sign of retreat, and did not do any injury to the Spaniards. The army-master sent me notice of this the same night, so that on the next day I started with as good order as I could, for we were in such great need of food that I thought we should all die of hunger if we continued to be without provisions for another day, especially the Indians, since altogether we did not have two bushels of corn, and so I was obliged to hasten forward without delay. The Indians lighted their fires from point to point, and these were answered from a distance with as good understanding as we could have shown. Thus notice was given concerning how we went and where we had arrived.

As soon as I came within sight of this city, I sent the army-master, Don Garcia Lopez, Friar Daniel and Friar Luis, and Ferrando Vermizzo, with some horsemen, a little way ahead, so that they might find the Indians and tell them that we were not coming to do them any harm, but to defend them in the name of our lord the Emperor. The summons, in the form which His Majesty commanded in his instructions, was made intelligible to the people of the country by an interpreter. But they, being a proud people, were little affected, because it seemed to them that we were few in number, and that they would not have any difficulty in conquering us. They pierced the gown of Friar Luis with an arrow, which, blessed be God, did him no harm. Meanwhile I arrived with all the rest of the horse and the footmen, and found a large body of the Indians on the plain, who began to shoot with their arrows. In obedience to the orders of Your Lordship and of the marquis,[1] I did not wish my company, who were begging me for permission, to attack them, telling them that they ought not to offend them, and that what the enemy was doing was nothing, and that so few people ought not to be insulted. On the other hand, when the Indians saw that we did not move, they took greater courage, and grew so bold that they came up almost to the heels of our horses to shoot their arrows. On this account I saw that it was no longer time to hesitate, and as the priests approved the action, I charged them. There was little to do, because they suddenly took to flight, part running toward the city, which was near and well fortified, and others toward the plain, wherever chance led them. Some Indians were killed, and others might have been slain if I could have allowed them to be pursued. But I saw that there would be little advantage in this, because the Indians who were outside were few, and those who had retired to the city were numerous, besides many who had remained there in the first place.

As that was where the food was, of which

---

[1] It is possible that this is a blunder, in Ramusio's text, for "His Majesty." The Marquis, in New Spain, is always Cortes, for whom neither Mendoza nor Coronado had any especial regard.

we stood in such great need, I assembled
my whole force and divided them as seemed
to me best for the attack on the city, and
surrounded it. The hunger which we suffered
would not permit of any delay, and so I dismounted with some of these gentlemen and
soldiers. I ordered the musketeers and
crossbowmen to begin the attack and drive
back the enemy from the defenses, so that
they could not do us any injury. I assaulted the wall on one side, where I was
told that there was a scaling ladder and that
there was also a gate. But the crossbowmen broke all the strings of their crossbows
and the musketeers could do nothing, because they had arrived so weak and feeble
that they could scarcely stand on their feet.
On this account the people who were on
top were not prevented at all from defending
themselves and doing us whatever injury
they were able. Thus, for myself, they
knocked me down to the ground twice with
countless great stones which they threw
down from above, and if I had not been protected by the very good headpiece which I
wore, I think that the outcome would have
been bad for me. They picked me up from
the ground, however, with two small wounds
in my face and an arrow in my foot, and
with many bruises on my arms and legs, and
in this condition I retired from the battle,
very weak. I think that if Don Garcia
Lopez de Cardenas had not come to my help,
like a good cavalier, the second time that

they knocked me to the ground, by placing his own body above mine, I should have been in much greater danger than I was. But, by the pleasure of God, these Indians surrendered, and their city was taken with the help of Our Lord, and a sufficient supply of corn was found there to relieve our necessities.

The army-master and Don Pedro de Tovar and Ferrando de Alvarado and Paulo de Melgosa, the infantry captain, sustained some bruises, although none of them were wounded. Agoniez Quarez was hit in the arm by an arrow, and one Torres, who lived in Panuco, in the face by another, and two other footmen received slight arrow wounds. They all directed their attack against me because my armor was gilded and glittered, and on this account I was hurt more than the rest, and not because I had done more or was farther in advance than the others; for all these gentlemen and soldiers bore themselves well, as was expected of them. I praise God that I am now well, although somewhat sore from the stones. Two or three other soldiers were hurt in the battle which we had on the plain, and three horses were killed—one that of Don Lopez and another that of Vigliega and the third that of Don Alfonso Manrich—and seven or eight other horses were wounded; but the men, as well as the horses, have now recovered and are well.

III

Of the situation and condition of the Seven Cities called the kingdom of Cevola, and the sort of people and their customs, and of the animals which are found there.

IT now remains for me to tell about this city and kingdom and province, of which the Father Provincial gave Your Lordship an account. In brief, I can assure you that in reality he has not told the truth in a single thing that he said, but everything is the reverse of what he said, except the name of the city and the large stone houses. For, although they are not decorated with turquoises, nor made of lime nor of good bricks, nevertheless they are very good houses, with three and four and five stories, where there are very good apartments and good rooms with corridors,[1] and some very good rooms under ground and paved, which are made for winter, and are something like a sort of hot baths.[2] The ladders which they have for their houses are all movable and portable, which are taken up and placed wherever they please. They are made of two pieces of wood, with rounds like ours.

The Seven Cities are seven little villages,

---

[1] Hakluyt: . . . "very excellent good houses of three or foure or fiue lofts high, wherein are good lodgings and faire chambers with lathers in stead of staires."

[2] The kivas or ceremonial chambers.

all having the kind of houses I have described. They are all within a radius of 5 leagues. They are all called the kingdom of Cevola, and each has its own name and no single one is called Cevola, but all together are called Cevola. This one which I have called a city I have named Granada, partly because it has some similarity to it, as well as out of regard for Your Lordship. In this place where I am now lodged there are perhaps 200 houses, all surrounded by a wall, and it seems to me that with the other houses, which are not so surrounded, there might be altogether 500 families. There is another town near by, which is one of the seven, but somewhat larger than this, and another of the same size as this, and the other four are somewhat smaller. I send them all to Your Lordship, painted with the route. The skin on which the painting is made was found here with other skins.

The people of the towns seem to me to be of ordinary size and intelligent, although I do not think that they have the judgment and intelligence which they ought to have to build these houses in the way in which they have, for most of them are entirely naked except the covering of their privy parts, and they have painted mantles like the one which I send to Your Lordship. They do not raise cotton, because the country is very cold, but they wear mantles, as may be seen by the exhibit which I send. It is also true that some cotton thread was

173

found in their houses. They wear the hair on their heads like the Mexicans. They all have good figures, and are well bred. I think that they have a quantity of turquoises, which they had removed with the rest of their goods, except the corn, when I arrived, because I did not find any women here nor any men under 15 years or over 60, except two or three old men who remained in command of all the other men and the warriors. Two points of emerald and some little broken stones which approach the color of rather poor garnets [1] were found in a paper, besides other stone crystals, which I gave to one of my servants to keep until they could be sent to Your Lordship. He has lost them, as they tell me. We found fowls, but only a few, and yet there are some. The Indians tell me that they do not eat these in any of the seven villages, but that they keep them merely for the sake of procuring the feathers.[2] I do not believe this, because they are very good, and better than those of Mexico.

The climate of this country and the temperature of the air is almost like that of Mexico, because it is sometimes hot and sometimes it rains. I have not yet seen it rain, however, except once when there fell a little shower with wind, such as often falls

[1] Many garnets are found on the ant-hills throughout the region, especially in the Navajo country.

[2] The natives doubtless told the truth. Eagle and turkey feathers are still highly prized by them for use in their ceremonies.

in Spain. The snow and the cold are usually very great, according to what the natives of the country all say. This may very probably be so, both because of the nature of the country and the sort of houses they build and the skins and other things which these people have to protect them from the cold. There are no kinds of fruit or fruit trees. The country is all level, and is nowhere shut in by high mountains, although there are some hills and rough passages.[1] There are not many birds, probably because of the cold, and because there are no mountains near. There are no trees fit for firewood here, because they can bring enough for their needs from a clump of very small cedars 4 leagues distant.[2] Very good grass is found a quarter of a league away, where there is pasturage for our horses as well as mowing for hay, of which we had great need, because our horses were so weak and feeble when they arrived.

The food which they eat in this country is corn, of which they have a great abundance, and beans and venison, which they probably eat (although they say that they do not), because we found many skins of deer and hares and rabbits. They make the best

[1] It should be noted that Coronado clearly distinguishes between hills or mesas and mountains. Zuñi valley is hemmed in by heights varying from 500 to 1,000 feet.
[2] This accords perfectly with the condition of the vegetation in Zuñi valley at the present time.

corn cakes I have ever seen anywhere, and this is what everybody ordinarily eats. They have the very best arrangement and machinery for grinding that was ever seen [plate LXIV]. One of these Indian women here will grind as much as four of the Mexicans. They have very good salt in crystals, which they bring from a lake a day's journey distant from here. No information can be obtained among them about the North sea or that on the west, nor do I know how to tell Your Lordship which we are nearest to. I should judge that it is nearer to the western, and 150 leagues is the nearest that it seems to me it can be thither. The North sea ought to be much farther away. Your Lordship may thus see how very wide the country is. They have many animals—bears, tigers, lions, porcupines, and some sheep as big as a horse, with very large horns and little tails. I have seen some of their horns the size of which was something to marvel at. There are also wild goats, whose heads I have seen, and the paws of the bears and the skins of the wild boars. For game they have deer, leopards, and very large deer,[1] and every one thinks that some of them are larger than that animal which Your Lordship favored me with, which belonged to Juan Melaz. They inhabit some plains eight days' journey toward the north. They have some of their skins here very well dressed,

[1] Doubtless a slip of Ramusio's pen for cows, i. e., buffalos.

and they prepare and paint them where they kill the cows, according to what they tell me.

IV

Of the nature and situation of the kingdoms of Totonteac, Marata, and Acus, wholly different from the account of Friar Marcos. The conference which they had with the Indians of the city of Granada, which they had captured, who had been forewarned of the coming of Christians into their country fifty years before. The account which was obtained from them concerning seven other cities, of which Tucano is the chief, and how he sent to discover them. A present sent to Mendoza of various things found in this country by Vazquez Coronado.

THESE Indians say that the kingdom of Totonteac, which the father provincial praised so much, saying that it was something marvelous, and of such a very great size, and that cloth was made there, is a hot lake, on the edge of which there are five or six houses.[1] There used to be some others, but these have been destroyed by war. The kingdom of Marata can not be found, nor do these Indians know anything about it. The kingdom of Acus is a single small city, where they raise cotton, and this is called Acucu.[2] I say that this is the country, because Acus, with or without the aspiration, is not a word

[1] Coronado doubtless misinterpreted what the natives intended to communicate. The "hot lake" was in all probability the salt lake alluded to on page 154, near which Marata was situated. Totonteac was of course Tusayan, or "Tucano."

[2] This is a form of the Zuñi name for Acoma—Hakukia.

in this region; and because it seems to me that Acucu may be derived from Acus, I say that it is this town which has been converted into the kingdom of Acus. They tell me that there are some other small ones not far from this settlement, which are situated on a river which I have seen and of which the Indians have told me. God knows that I wish I had better news to write to Your Lordship, but I must give you the truth, and, as I wrote you from Culiacan, I must advise you of the good as well as of the bad. But you may be assured that if there had been all the riches and treasures of the world, I could not have done more in His Majesty's service and in that of Your Lordship than I have done, in coming here where you commanded me to go, carrying, both my companions and myself, our food on our backs for 300 leagues, and traveling on foot many days, making our way over hills and rough mountains, besides other labors which I refrain from mentioning. Nor do I think of stopping until my death, if it serves His Majesty or Your Lordship to have it so.

Three days after I captured this city, some of the Indians who lived here came to offer to make peace. They brought me some turquoises and poor mantles, and I received them in His Majesty's name with as good a speech as I could, making them understand the purpose of my coming to this country, which is, in the name of His Majesty and by the commands of Your Lordship, that

they and all others in this province should
become Christians and should know the true
God for their Lord, and His Majesty for
their king and earthly lord.   After this they
returned to their houses and suddenly, the
next day, they packed up their goods and
property, their women and children, and
fled to the hills, leaving their towns deserted,
with only some few remaining in them.
Seeing this, I went to the town which I said
was larger than this, eight or ten days later,
when I had recovered from my wounds.   I
found a few of them there, whom I told that
they ought not to feel any fear, and I asked
them to summon their lord to me.   By
what I can find out or observe, however,
none of these towns have any, since I have
not seen any principal house by which any
superiority over others could be shown.[1]
Afterward, an old man, who said he was
their lord, came with a mantle made of many
pieces, with whom I argued as long as he
stayed with me.   He said that he would
come to see me with the rest of the chiefs of
the country, three days later, in order to
arrange the relations which should exist between us.   He did so, and they brought me
some little ragged mantles and some tur-

[1] As clear a description of the form of tribal government among the Pueblo Indians as is anywhere
to be found is in Bandelier's story, The Delight
Makers.   Mr. Bandelier has been most successful in
his effort to picture the actions and spirit of Indian
life.

179

quoises. I said that they ought to come down from their strongholds and return to their houses with their wives and children, and that they should become Christians, and recognize His Majesty as their king and lord. But they still remain in their strongholds, with their wives and all their property.

I commanded them to have a cloth painted for me, with all the animals that they know in that country, and although they are poor painters, they quickly painted two for me, one of the animals and the other of the birds and fishes. They say that they will bring their children so that our priests may instruct them, and that they desire to know our law. They declare that it was foretold among them more than fifty years ago that a people such as we are should come, and the direction they should come from, and that the whole country would be conquered. So far as I can find out, the water is what these Indians worship, because they say that it makes the corn grow and sustains their life, and that the only other reason they know is because their ancestors did so.[1] I have tried in every way to find out from the natives of these settlements whether they know of any other peoples or provinces or

[1] Dr. J. Walter Fewkes has conclusively shown that the snake dance, probably the most dramatic of Indian ceremonials, is essentially a prayer for rain. Coming as it does just as the natural rainy season approaches, the prayer is almost invariably answered.

cities. They tell me about seven cities which are at a considerable distance, which are like these, except that the houses there are not like these, but are made of earth [adobe], and small, and that they raise much cotton there. The first of these four places about which they know is called, they say, Tucano. They could not tell me much about the others. I do not believe that they tell me the truth, because they think that I shall soon have to depart from them and return home. But they will quickly find that they are deceived in this. I sent Don Pedro de Tobar there, with his company and some other horsemen, to see it. I would not have dispatched this packet to Your Lordship until I had learned what he found there, if I thought that I should have any news from him within twelve or fifteen days. However, as he will remain away at least thirty, and, considering that this information is of little importance and that the cold and the rains are approaching, it seemed to me that I ought to do as Your Lordship commanded me in your instructions, which is, that as soon as I arrived here, I should advise you thereof, and this I do, by sending you the plain narrative of what I have seen, which is bad enough, as you may perceive. I have determined to send throughout all the surrounding regions, in order to find out whether there is anything, and to suffer every extremity before I give up this enterprise, and to serve His Majesty, if I can find

any way in which to do it, and not to lack
in diligence until Your Lordship directs me
as to what I ought to do.

We have great need of pasture, and you
should know, also, that among all those who
are here there is not one pound of raisins,
nor sugar, nor oil, nor wine, except barely
half a quart, which is saved to say mass,
since everything is consumed, and part was
lost on the way. Now, you can provide us
with what appears best; but if you are thinking of sending us cattle, you should know
that it will be necessary for them to spend
at least a year on the road, because they can
not come in any other way, nor any quicker.
I would have liked to send to Your Lordship, with this dispatch, many samples of
the things which they have in this country,
but the trip is so long and rough that it is
difficult for me to do so. However, I send
you twelve small mantles, such as the people
of this country ordinarily wear, and a garment which seems to me to be very well
made. I kept it because it seemed to me to
be of very good workmanship, and because I
do not think that anyone has ever seen in
these Indies any work done with a needle,
unless it were done since the Spaniards settled here. And I also send two cloths
painted with the animals which they have
in this country, although, as I said, the
painting is very poorly done, because the
artist did not spend more than one day in
painting it. I have seen other paintings on

the walls of these houses which have much
better proportion and are done much better.

I send you a cow skin, some turquoises,
and two earrings of the same, and fifteen of
the Indian combs,[1] and some plates decorated with these turquoises, and two baskets
made of wicker, of which the Indians have
a large supply. I also send two rolls, such
as the women usually wear on their heads
when they bring water from the spring, the
same way that they do in Spain. One of
these Indian women, with one of these rolls
on her head, will carry a jar of water up a
ladder without touching it with her hands.
And, lastly, I send you samples of the weapons with which the natives of this country
fight, a shield, a hammer, and a bow with
some arrows, among which there are two
with bone points, the like of which have
never been seen, according to what these
conquerors say. As far as I can judge, it
does not appear to me that there is any hope
of getting gold or silver, but I trust in God
that, if there is any, we shall get our share
of it, and it shall not escape us through any
lack of diligence in the search.[2] I am unable to give Your Lordship any certain information about the dress of the women,
because the Indians keep them guarded so

[1] Possibly those used in weaving.
[2] The conquerors, in the literature of New Spain,
are almost always those who shared with Cortes in
the labors and the glory of the Spanish conquest of
Mexico.

carefully that I have not seen any, except two old women. These had on two long skirts reaching down to their feet and open in front, and a girdle, and they are tied together with some cotton strings. I asked the Indians to give me one of those which they wore, to send to you, since they were not willing to show me the women. They brought me two mantles, which are these that I send, almost painted over. They have two tassels, like the women of Spain, which hang somewhat over their shoulders.

The death of the negro is perfectly certain, because many of the things which he wore have been found, and the Indians say that they killed him here because the Indians of Chichilticale said that he was a bad man, and not like the Christians, because the Christians never kill women, and he killed them, and because he assaulted their women, whom the Indians love better than themselves. Therefore they determined to kill him, but they did not do it in the way that was reported, because they did not kill any of the others who came with him, nor did they kill the lad from the province of Petatlan, who was with him, but they took him and kept him in safe custody until now. When I tried to secure him, they made excuses for not giving him to me, for two or three days, saying that he was dead, and at other times that the Indians of Acucu had taken him away. But when I finally told them that I should be very angry if they did not give him to me, they gave him to me. He is an interpreter; for although he can not talk much, he understands very well.

Some gold and silver has been found in this place, which those who know about minerals say is not bad. I have not yet been able to learn from these people where they got it. I perceive that they refuse to tell me the truth in everything, because they think that I shall have to depart from here in a short time, as I have said. But I trust in God that they will not be able to avoid answering much longer. I beg Your Lordship to make a report of the success of this expedition to His Majesty, because there is nothing more than what I have already said. I shall not do so until it shall please God to grant that we find what we desire. Our Lord God protect and keep your most illustrious Lordship. From the province of Cevola, and this city of Granada, the 3d of August, 1540. Francisco Vazquez de Coronado kisses the hand of your most illustrious Lordship.

TRANSLATION OF THE TRASLADO DE LAS NUEVAS [1]

COPY OF THE REPORTS AND DESCRIPTIONS
THAT HAVE BEEN RECEIVED REGARDING
THE DISCOVERY OF A CITY WHICH IS
CALLED CIBOLA, SITUATED IN THE NEW
COUNTRY.

HIS grace left the larger part of his army
in the valley of Culiacan, and with only 75
companions on horseback and 30 footmen,
he set out for here Thursday, April 22. The
army which remained there was to start
about the end of the month of May, because
they could not find any sort of sustenance
for the whole of the way that they had to
go, as far as this province of Cibola, which
is 350 long leagues, and on this account he
did not dare to put the whole army on the
road. As for the men he took with him, he
ordered them to make provision for eighty
days, which was carried on horses, each having one for himself and his followers. With
very great danger of suffering hunger, and

[1] Translated from Pacheco y Cardenas, Documentos de Indias, vol. xix., p. 529. This document is
anonymous, but it is evidently a copy of a letter
from some trusted companion, written from Granada-
Hawikuh, about the time of Coronado's letter of
August 3, 1540. In the title to the document as
printed, the date is given as 1531, but there can be
no doubt that it is an account of Coronado's journey.

not less labor, since they had to open the way, and every day discovered waterways and rivers with bad crossings, they stood it after a fashion, and on the whole journey as far as this province there was not a peck of corn.

He reached this province on Wednesday, the 7th of July last, with all the men whom he led from the valley very well, praise be to Our Lord, except one Spaniard who died of hunger four days from here and some negroes and Indians who also died of hunger and thirst. The Spaniard was one of those on foot, and was named Espinosa. In this way his grace spent seventy-seven days on the road before reaching here, during which God knows in what sort of a way we lived, and whether we could have eaten much more than we ate the day that his grace reached this city of Granada, for so it has been named out of regard for the viceroy, and because they say it resembles the Albaicin.[1] The force he led was not received the way it should have been, because they all arrived very tired from the great labor of the journey. This, and the loading and unloading like so many muleteers, and not eating as much as they should have, left them more in need of resting several days than of fighting, although there was not a man in the

[1] A part of Granada, near the Alhambra. There is a curious similarity in the names Albaicin and Hawikuh, the latter being the native name of Coronado's Granada.

army who would not have done his best in everything if the horses, who suffered the same as their masters, could have helped them.

The city was deserted by men over sixty years and under twenty, and by women and children. All who were there were the fighting men who remained to defend the city, and many of them came out, about a crossbow shot, uttering loud threats. The general himself went forward with two priests and the army-master, to urge them to surrender, as is the custom in new countries. The reply that he received was from many arrows which they let fly, and they wounded Hernando Bermejo's horse and pierced the loose flap of the frock of father Friar Luis, the former companion of the Lord Bishop of Mexico. When this was seen, taking as their advocate the Holy Saint James,[1] he rushed upon them with all his force, which he had kept in very good order, and although the Indians turned their backs and tried to reach the city, they were overtaken and many of them killed before they could reach it. They killed three horses and wounded seven or eight.

When my lord the general reached the city, he saw that it was surrounded by stone walls, and the houses very high, four and five and even six stories apiece, with their flat roofs and balconies. As the Indians

[1] Uttering the war cry of Santiago.

had made themselves secure within it, and
would not let anyone come near without
shooting arrows at him, and as we could not
obtain anything to eat unless we captured
it, his grace decided to enter the city on foot
and to surround it by men on horseback, so
that the Indians who were inside could not
get away. As he was distinguished among
them all by his gilt arms and a plume on
his headpiece, all the Indians aimed at him,
because he was noticeable among all, and
they knocked him down to the ground twice
by chance stones thrown from the flat roofs,
and stunned him in spite of his headpiece,
and if this had not been so good, I doubt if
he would have come out alive from that enterprise, and besides all this—praised be Our
Lord that he came out on his own feet—
they hit him many times with stones on his
head and shoulders and legs, and he received
two small wounds on his face and an arrow
wound in the right foot; but despite all this
his grace is as sound and well as the day he
left that city. And you[1] may assure my
lord of all this, and also that on the 19th of
July last he went 4 leagues from this city to
see a rock where they told him that the
Indians of this province had fortified themselves,[2] and he returned the same day, so that
he went 8 leagues in going and returning.

I think I have given you an account of

[1] The printed manuscript is V. M., which signifies
Your Majesty.
[2] Doubtless Thunder mountain.

everything, for it is right that I should be
the authority for you and his lordship, to
assure you that everything is going well with
the general my lord, and without any hesita-
tion I can assure you that he is as well and
sound as the day he left the city. He is
located within the city, for when the Indians
saw that his grace was determined to enter
the city, then they abandoned it, since they
let them go with their lives. We found in
it what we needed more than gold and silver, and that was much corn and beans and
fowls, better than those of New Spain, and
salt, the best and whitest that I have seen
in all my life.

THIS IS THE LATEST ACCOUNT OF CIBOLA, AND OF MORE THAN FOUR HUNDRED LEAGUES BEYOND.[1]

IT is more than 300 leagues from Culiacan to Cibola, uninhabited most of the way.
There are very few people there; the country is sterile; the roads are very bad. The
people go around entirely naked, except the
women, who wear white tanned deer skins
from the waist down, something like little
skirts, reaching to the feet. Their houses

[1] From a manuscript in the possession of the family of the late Sr. D. Joaquin Garcia Icazbalceta, of
the City of Mexico. This appears to be a transcript
from letters written, probably at Tiguex, on the Rio
Grande, during the late summer or early fall of
1541.

are of mats made of reeds; the houses are round and small, so that there is hardly room inside for a man on his feet. The country is sandy where they live near together and where they plant. They raise corn, but not very much, and beans and melons, and they also live on game—rabbits, hares, and deer. They do not have sacrifices. This is between Culiacan and Cibola.

Cibola is a village of about 200 houses. They have two and three and four and five stories. The walls are about a handbreadth thick; the sticks of timber are as large as the wrist, and round; for boards, they have very small bushes, with their leaves on, covered with a sort of greenish-colored mud; the walls are of dirt and mud, the doors of the houses are like the hatchways of ships. The houses are close together, each joined to the others. Outside of the houses they have some hot-houses (or estufas) of dirt mud, where they take refuge from the cold in the winter—because this is very great, since it snows six months in the year.

Some of these people wear cloaks of cotton and of the maguey (or Mexican aloe) and of tanned deer skin, and they wear shoes made of these skins, reaching up to the knees. They also make cloaks of the skins of hares and rabbits, with which they cover themselves. The women wear cloaks of the maguey, reaching down to the feet, with girdles; they wear their hair gathered about the ears like little wheels. They raise corn

and beans and melons, which is all they
need to live on, because it is a small tribe.
The land where they plant is entirely sandy;
the water is brackish; the country is very
dry. They have some fowls, although not
many. They do not know what sort of a
thing fish is. There are seven villages in
this province of Cibola within a space of 5
leagues; the largest may have about 200
houses and two others about 200, and the
others somewhere between 60 or 50 and 30
houses.

It is 60 leagues from Cibola to the river
and province of Tibex [Tiguex]. The first
village is 40 leagues from Cibola, and is
called Acuco. This village is on top of a
very strong rock; it has about 200 houses,
built in the same way as at Cibola, where
they speak another language. It is 20
leagues from here to the river of Tiguex.
The river is almost as wide as that of
Seville, although not so deep; it flows
through a level country; the water is good;
it contains some fish; it rises in the north.
He who relates this, saw twelve villages
within a certain distance of the river; others
saw more, they say, up the river. Below,
all the villages are small, except two that
have about 200 houses. The walls of these
houses are something like mud walls of dirt
and sand, very rough; they are as thick as
the breadth of a hand. The houses have
two and three stories; the construction is
like those at Cibola. The country is very

cold. They have hot-houses, as in Cibola, and the river freezes so thick that loaded animals cross it, and it would be possible for carts to do so. They raise as much corn as they need, and beans and melons. They have some fowls, which they keep so as to make cloaks of their feathers. They raise cotton, although not much; they wear cloaks made of this, and shoes of hide, as at Cibola. These people defend themselves very well, and from within their houses, since they do not care to come out. The country is all sandy.

Four days' journey from the province and river of Tiguex four villages are found. The first has 30 houses; the second is a large village destroyed in their wars, and has about 35 houses occupied; the third about

These three are like those at the river in every way. The fourth is a large village which is among some mountains. It is called Cicuic, and has about 50 houses, with as many stories as those at Cibola. The walls are of dirt and mud like those at Cibola. It has plenty of corn, beans and melons, and some fowls. Four days from this village they came to a country as level as the sea, and in these plains there was such a multitude of cows that they are numberless. These cows are like those of Castile, and somewhat larger, as they have a little hump on the withers, and they are more reddish, approaching black; their hair, more than a span long, hangs down around their horns and ears and chin, and along the neck and shoulders like manes, and down from the knees; all the rest is a very fine wool, like merino; they have very good, tender meat, and much fat.

Having proceeded many days through these plains, they came to a settlement of about 200 inhabited houses. The houses were made of the skins of the cows, tanned white, like pavilions or army tents. The maintenance or sustenance of these Indians comes entirely from the cows, because they neither sow nor reap corn. With the skins they make their houses, with the skins they clothe and shoe themselves, of the skins they make rope, and also of the wool; from the sinews they make thread, with which they sew their clothes and also their houses; from the bones they make awls; the dung serves them for wood, because there is nothing else in that country; the stomachs serve them for pitchers and vessels from which they drink; they live on the flesh; they sometimes eat it half roasted and warmed over the dung, at other times raw; seizing it with their fingers, they pull it out with one hand and with a flint knife in the other they cut off mouthfuls, and thus swallow it half chewed; they eat the fat raw, without warming it; they drink the blood just as it leaves the cows, and at other times after it has run out, cold and raw; they have no other means of livelihood.

These people have dogs like those in this

country, except that they are somewhat larger, and they load these dogs like beasts of burden, and make saddles for them like our pack saddles, and they fasten them with their leather thongs, and these make their backs sore on the withers like pack animals. When they go hunting, they load these with their necessities, and when they move—for these Indians are not settled in one place, since they travel wherever the cows move, to support themselves—these dogs carry their houses, and they have the sticks of their houses dragging along tied on to the pack-saddles, besides the load which they carry on top, and the load may be, according to the dog, from 35 to 50 pounds. It is 30 leagues, or even more, from Cibola to these plains where they went. The plains stretch away beyond, nobody knows how far. The captain, Francisco Vazquez, went farther across the plains, with 30 horsemen, and Friar Juan de Padilla with him; all the rest of the force returned to the settlement at the river to wait for Francisco Vazquez, because this was his command. It is not known whether he has returned.

The country is so level that men became lost when they went off half a league. One horseman was lost, who never reappeared, and two horses, all saddled and bridled, which they never saw again. No track was left of where they went, and on this account it was necessary to mark the road by which they went with cow dung, so as to return,

since there were no stones or anything
else.

Marco Polo, the Venetian, in his treatise,
in chapter 15, relates and says that (he saw)
the same cows, with the same sort of hump;
and in the same chapter he says that there
are sheep as big as horses.

Nicholas, the Venetian, gave an account
to Micer Pogio, the Florentine, in his second
book, toward the end, which says that in
Ethiopia there are oxen with a hump, like
camels, and they have horns 3 cubits long,
and they carry their horns up over their
backs, and one of these horns makes a wine
pitcher.

Marco Polo, in chapter 134, says that in
the country of the Tartars, toward the north,
they have dogs as large or little smaller than
asses. They harness these into a sort of
cart and with these enter a very miry country, all a quagmire, where other animals can
not enter and come out without getting
submerged, and on this account they take
dogs.

TRANSLATION OF THE RELACION DEL SUCESO [1]

ACCOUNT OF WHAT HAPPENED ON THE JOURNEY WHICH FRANCISCO VAZQUEZ MADE TO DISCOVER CIBOLA.

WHEN the army reached the valley of Culiacan, Francisco Vazquez divided the army on account of the bad news which was received regarding Cibola, and because the food supply along the way was small, according to the report of Melchor Diaz, who had just come back from seeing it. He himself took 80 horsemen and 25 foot soldiers, and a small part of the artillery, and set out from Culiacan, leaving Don Tristan de Arellano with the rest of the force, with orders to set out twenty days later, and when he reached the Valley of Hearts (Corazones) to wait there for a letter from him, which would be sent after he had reached

[1] The Spanish text of this document is printed in Buckingham Smith's Florida, p. 147, from a copy made by Muñoz, and also in Pacheco y Cardenas, Documentos de Indias, vol. xiv., p. 318, from a copy found in the Archives of the Indies at Seville. No date is given in the document, but there can be no doubt that it refers to Coronado's expedition. In the heading to the document in the Pacheco y Cardenas Coleccion, the date is given as 1531, and it is placed under that year in the chronologic index of the Coleccion.

Cibola, and had seen what was there; and this was done. The Valley of Hearts is 150 leagues from the valley of Culiacan, and the same distance from Cibola.

This whole distance, up to about 50 leagues before reaching Cibola, is inhabited, although it is away from the road in some places. The population is all of the same sort of people, since the houses are all of palm mats, and some of them have low lofts. They all have corn, although not much, and in some places very little. They have melons and beans. The best settlement of all is a valley called Señora, which is 10 leagues beyond the Hearts, where a town was afterward settled. There is some cotton among these, but deer skins are what most of them use for clothes.

Francisco Vazquez passed by all these on account of the small crops. There was no corn the whole way, except at this valley of Señora, where they collected a little, and besides this he had what he took from Culiacan, where he provided himself for eighty days. In seventy-three days we reached Cibola, although after hard labor and the loss of many horses and the death of several Indians, and after we saw it these were all doubled, although we did find corn enough. We found the natives peaceful for the whole way.

The day we reached the first village part of them came out to fight us, and the rest stayed in the village and fortified themselves.

It was not possible to make peace with these, although we tried hard enough, so it was necessary to attack them and kill some of them. The rest then drew back to the village, which was then surrounded and attacked. We had to withdraw, on account of the great damage they did us from the flat roofs, and we began to assault them from a distance with the artillery and muskets, and that afternoon they surrendered. Francisco Vazquez came out of it badly hurt by some stones, and I am certain, indeed, that he would have been there yet if it had not been for the army-master, D. Garcia Loper de Cardenas, who rescued him. When the Indians surrendered, they abandoned the village and went to the other villages, and as they left the houses we made ourselves at home in them.

Father Friar Marcos understood, or gave to understand, that the region and neighborhood in which there are seven villages was a single village which he called Cibola, but the whole of this settled region is called Cibola. The villages have from 150 to 200 and 300 houses; some have the houses of the village all together, although in some villages they are divided into two or three sections, but for the most part they are all together, and their courtyards are within, and in these are their hot rooms for winter, and they have their summer ones outside the villages. The houses have two or three stories, the walls of stone and mud, and some have mud walls. The villages have for the most part the walls of the houses; the houses are too good for Indians, especially for these, since they are brutish and have no decency in anything except in their houses.

For food they have much corn and beans and melons, and some fowls, like those of Mexico, and they keep these more for their feathers than to eat, because they make long robes of them, since they do not have any cotton; and they wear cloaks of heniquen (a fibrous plant), and of the skins of deer, and sometimes of cows.

Their rites and sacrifices are somewhat idolatrous, but water is what they worship most, to which they offer small painted sticks and feathers and yellow powder made of flowers, and usually this offering is made to springs. Sometimes, also, they offer such turquoises as they have, although poor ones.

From the valley of Culiacan to Cibola it is 240 leagues in two directions. It is north to about the thirty-fourth-and-a-half degree, and from there to Cibola, which is nearly the thirty-seventh degree, toward the north-east.

Having talked with the natives of Cibola about what was beyond, they said that there were settlements toward the west. Francisco Vazquez then sent Don Pedro de Tobar to investigate, who found seven other villages, which were called the province of Tuzan; this is 35 leagues to the west. The villages are somewhat larger than those of

Cibola, and in other respects, in food and everything, they are of the same sort, except that these raise cotton. While Don Pedro de Tobar had gone to see these, Francisco Vazquez dispatched messengers to the viceroy, with an account of what had happened up to this point.[1] He also prepared instructions for these to take to Don Tristan, who as I have said, was at Hearts, for him to proceed to Cibola, and to leave a town established in the valley of Señora, which he did, and in it he left 80 horsemen of the men who had but one horse and the weakest men, and Melchor Diaz with them as captain and leader, because Francisco Vazquez had so arranged for it. He ordered him to go from there with half the force to explore toward the west; and he did so, and traveled 150 leagues, to the river which Hernando de Alarcon entered from the sea, which he called the Buenaguia. The settlements and people that are in this direction are mostly like those at the Hearts, except at the river and around it, where the people have much better figures and have more corn, although the houses in which they live are hovels, like pig pens, almost under ground, with a covering of straw, and made without any skill whatever. This river is reported to be large. They reached it 30 leagues from the coast, where, and as far again above, Alarcon had come up with his boats two months be-

[1] See the letter of August 3, 1540.

fore they reached it. This river runs north and south there. Melchor Diaz passed on toward the west five or six days, from which he returned for the reason that he did not find any water or vegetation, but only many stretches of sand; and he had some fighting on his return to the river and its vicinity, because they wanted to take advantage of him while crossing the river. While returning Melchor Diaz died from an accident, by which he killed himself, throwing a lance at a dog.

After Don Pedro de Tobar returned and had given an account of those villages, he then dispatched Don Garcia Lopez de Cardenas, the army-master, by the same road Don Pedro had followed, to go beyond that province of Tuzan to the west, and he allowed him eighty days in which to go and return, for the journey and to make the discoveries. He was conducted beyond Tuzan by native guides, who said there were settlements beyond, although at a distance. Having gone 50 leagues west of Tuzan, and 80 from Cibola, he found the edge of a river down which it was impossible to find a path for a horse in any direction, or even for a man on foot, except in one very difficult place, where there was a descent for almost 2 leagues. The sides were such a steep rocky precipice that it was scarcely possible to see the river, which looks like a brook from above, although it is half as large again as that of Seville, according to what they say, so that although they sought for a passage with great diligence, none was found for a long distance, during which they were for several days in great need of water, which could not be found, and they could not approach that of the river, although they could see it, and on this account Don Garcia Lopez was forced to return. This river comes from the northeast and turns toward the south-southwest at the place where they found it, so that it is without any doubt the one that Melchor Diaz reached.

Four days after Francisco Vazquez had dispatched Don Garcia Lopez to make this discovery, he dispatched Hernando de Alvarado to explore the route toward the east. He started off, and 30 leagues from Cibola found a rock with a village on top, the strongest position that ever was seen in the world, which was called Acuco [1] in their language, and father Friar Marcos called it the kingdom of Hacus. They came out to meet us peacefully, although it would have been easy to decline to do this and to have stayed on their rock, where we would not have been able to trouble them. They gave us cloaks of cotton, skins of deer and of cows, and turquoises, and fowls and other food

[1] The Acoma people call their pueblo Áko, while the name for themselves is Akómĕ, signifying "people of the white rock." The Zuñi name of Acoma, as previously stated, is Hákukia; of the Acoma people, Háku-kwe. Hacus was applied by Niza to Hawikuh, not to Acoma—*Hodge.*

which they had, which is the same as in Cibola.

Twenty leagues to the east of this rock we found a river which runs north and south,[1] well settled; there are in all, small and large, 70 villages near it, a few more or less, the same sort as those at Cibola, except that they are almost all of well-made mud walls. The food is neither more nor less. They raise cotton—I mean those who live near the river—the others not. There is much corn here. These people do not have markets. They are settled for 50 leagues along this river, north and south, and some villages are 15 or 20 leagues distant, in one direction and the other. This river rises where these settlements end at the north, on the slope of the mountains there, where there is a larger village different from the others, called Yu-raba.[2] It is settled in this fashion: It has 18 divisions; each one has a situation as if for two ground plots; the houses are very close together, and have five or six stories, three of them with mud walls and two or three with thin wooden walls, which become smaller as they go up, and each one has its little balcony outside of the mud walls, one above the other, all around, of wood. In this village, as it is in the mountains, they do not raise cotton nor breed fowls; they

[1] The Rio Grande.
[2] Evidently Taos, the native name of which is Tŭatá, the Picuris name being Tuopá, according to Hodge.

204

wear the skins of deer and cows entirely.
It is the most populous village of all that
country; we estimated there were 15,000
souls in it. There is one of the other kind
of villages larger than all the rest, and very
strong, which is called Cicuique.[1] It has
four and five stories, has eight large courtyards, each one with its balcony, and there
are fine houses in it.

They do not raise cotton nor keep fowls,
because it is 15 leagues away from the river
to the east, toward the plains where the
cows are. After Alvarado had sent an account of this river to Francisco Vazquez, he
proceeded forward to these plains, and at the
borders of these he found a little river which
flows to the southwest, and after four days'
march he found the cows, which are the
most monstrous thing in the way of animals
which has ever been seen or read about.
He followed this river for 100 leagues, finding more cows every day. We provided
ourselves with some of these, although at
first, until we had had experience, at the
risk of the horses. There is such a quantity
of them that I do not know what to compare
them with, except with the fish in the sea,
because on this journey, as also on that
which the whole army afterward made when
it was going to Quivira, there were so many
that many times when we started to pass
through the midst of them and wanted to go

[1] Identical with Castañeda's Cicuyc or Cicuye—
the pueblo of Pecos.

through to the other side of them, we were not able to, because the country was covered with them. The flesh of these is as good as that of Castile, and some said it was even better.

The bulls are large and brave, although they do not attack very much; but they have wicked horns, and in a fight use them well, attacking fiercely; they killed several of our horses and wounded many. We found the pike to be the best weapon to use against them, and the musket for use when this misses.

When Hernando de Alvarado returned from these plains to the river which was called Tiguex, he found the army-master Don Garcia Lopez de Cardenas getting ready for the whole army, which was coming there. When it arrived, although all these people had met Hernando de Alvarado peacefully, part of them rebelled when all the force came. There were 12 villages near together, and one night they killed 40 of our horses and mules which were loose in the camp. They fortified themselves in their villages, and war was then declared against them. Don Garcia Lopez went to the first and took it and executed justice on many of them. When the rest saw this, they abandoned all except two of the villages, one of these the strongest one of all, around which the army was kept for two months. And although after we invested it, we entered it one day and occupied a part of the flat roof, we were forced to abandon this on account of the many wounds that were received and because it was so dangerous to maintain ourselves there, and although we again entered it soon afterward, in the end it was not possible to get it all, and so it was surrounded all this time. We finally captured it because of their thirst, and they held out so long because it snowed twice when they were just about to give themselves up. In the end we captured it, and many of them were killed because they tried to get away at night.

Francisco Vazquez obtained an account from some Indians who were found in this village of Cicuique, which, if it had been true, was of the richest thing that has been found in the Indies. The Indian who gave the news and the account came from a village called Harale, 300 leagues east of this river. He gave such a clear account of what he told, as if it was true and he had seen it, that it seemed plain afterward that it was the devil who was speaking in him. Francisco Vazquez and all of us placed much confidence in him, although he was advised by several gentlemen not to move the whole army, but rather to send a captain to find out what was there. He did not wish to do this, but wanted to take every one, and even to send Don Pedro de Tobar to the Hearts for half the men who were in that village. So he started with the whole army, and proceeded 150 leagues, 100 to the east and 50 to the south,[1] and the Indian failing to make good what he had said about there being a settlement there, and corn, with which to proceed farther, the other two guides were asked how that was, and one confessed that what the Indian said was a lie, except that there was a province which was called Quivira, and that there was corn and houses of straw there, but that they were very far off, because we had been led astray a distance from the road. Considering this, and the small supply of food that was left, Francisco Vazquez, after consulting with the captains, determined to proceed with 30 of the best men who were well equipped, and that the army should return to the river; and this was done at once. Two days before this, Don Garcia Lopez' horse had happened to fall with him, and he threw his arm out of joint, from which he suffered much, and so Don Tristan de Arellano returned to the river with the army. On this journey they had a very hard time, because almost all of them had nothing to eat except meat, and many suffered on this account. They killed a world of bulls and cows, for there were days when they brought 60 and 70 head into camp, and it was necessary to go hunting every day, and on this account, and from not eating any corn during all this time, the horses suffered much.

Francisco Vazquez set out across these

[1] Southeast, in Buckingham Smith's Muñoz copy.

plains in search of Quivira, more on account of the story which had been told us at the river than from the confidence which was placed in the guide here, and after proceeding many days by the needle (i. e., to the north) it pleased God that after thirty days' march we found the river Quivira, which is 30 leagues below the settlement. While going up the valley, we found people who were going hunting, who were natives of Quivira.

All that there is at Quivira is a very brutish people, without any decency whatever in their houses nor in anything. These are of straw, like the Tarascan settlements; in some villages there are as many as 200 houses; they have corn and beans and melons; they do not have cotton nor fowls, nor do they make bread which is cooked, except under the ashes. Francisco Vazquez went 25 leagues through these settlements, to where he obtained an account of what was beyond, and they said that the plains come to an end, and that down the river there are people who do not plant, but live wholly by hunting.

They also gave an account of two other large villages, one of which was called Tareque [1] and the other Arae, with straw houses at Tareque, and at Arae some of straw and some of skins. Copper was found here, and they said it came from a distance.

[1] Tuxeque, in the Muñoz copy.

From what the Indian had said, it is possible that this village of Arae contains more,[1] from the clear description of it which he gave. We did not find any trace or news of it here. Francisco Vazquez returned from here to the river of Tiguex, where he found the army. We went back by a more direct route, because in going by the way we went we traveled 330 leagues, and it is not more than 200 by that by which we returned. Quivira is in the fortieth degree and the river in the thirty-sixth. It was so dangerous to travel or to go away from the camp in these plains, that it is as if one was traveling on the sea, since the only roads are those of the cows, and they are so level and have no mountain or prominent landmark, that if one went out of sight of it, he was lost, and in this way we lost one man, and others who went hunting wandered around two or three days, lost.

Two kinds of people travel around these plains with the cows; one is called Querechos and the others Teyas; they are very well built, and painted, and are enemies of each other. They have no other settlement or location than comes from traveling around with the cows. They kill all of these they wish, and tan the hides, with which they clothe themselves and make their tents, and they eat the flesh, sometimes even raw, and they also even drink the blood when thirsty. The tents they make are like field tents, and

[1] Or mines, as Muñoz guesses.

they set them up over some poles they have made for this purpose, which come together and are tied at the top, and when they go from one place to another they carry them on some dogs they have, of which they have many, and they load them with the tents and poles and other things, for the country is so level, as I said, that they can make use of these, because they carry the poles dragging along on the ground. The sun is what they worship most. The skin for the tents is cured on both sides, without the hair, and they have the skins of deer and cows left over.[1] They exchange some cloaks with the natives of the river for corn.

After Francisco Vazquez reached the river, where he found the army, Don Pedro de Tobar came with half the people from the Hearts, and Don Garcia Lopez de Cardenas started off for Mexico, who, besides the fact that his arm was very bad, had permission from the viceroy on account of the death of his brother. Ten or twelve who were sick went with him, and not a man among them all who could fight. He reached the town of the Spaniards and found it burned and two Spaniards and many Indians and horses dead, and he returned to the river on this account, escaping from them by good fortune and great exertions. The cause of this misfortune was that after Don Pedro started and left 40 men there, half of these raised a mu-

[1] And jerked beef dried in the sun, in the Muñoz copy only.

tiny and fled, and the Indians, who remembered the bad treatment they had received, attacked them one night and overpowered them because of their carelessness and weakness, and they fled to Culiacan. Francisco Vazquez fell while running a horse about this time and was sick a long time, and after the winter was over he determined to come back, and although they may say something different, he did so, because he wanted to do this more than anything, and so we all came together as far as Culiacan, and each one went where he pleased from there, and Francisco Vazquez came here to Mexico to make his report to the viceroy, who was not at all pleased with his coming, although he pretended so at first. He was pleased that Father Friar Juan de Padilla had stayed there, who went to Quivira, and a Spaniard and a negro with him, and Friar Luis, a very holy lay brother, stayed in Cicuique. We spent two very cold winters at this river, with much snow and thick ice. The river froze one night and remained so for more than a month, so that loaded horses crossed on the ice. The reason these villages are settled in this fashion is supposed to be the great cold, although it is also partly the wars which they have with one another. And this is all that was seen and found out about all that country, which is very barren of fruits and groves. Quivira is a better country, having many huts and not being so cold, although it is more to the north.

TRANSLATION OF A LETTER FROM CORONADO TO THE KING, OCTOBER 20, 1541 [1]

LETTERS FROM FRANCISCO VAZQUEZ CORONADO TO HIS MAJESTY, IN WHICH HE GIVES AN ACCOUNT OF THE DISCOVERY OF THE PROVINCE OF TIGUEX.

HOLY CATHOLIC CÆSARIAN MAJESTY: On April 20 of this year I wrote to Your Majesty from this province of Tiguex, in reply to a letter from Your Majesty dated in Madrid, June 11 a year ago. I gave a detailed account of this expedition, which the viceroy of New Spain ordered me to undertake in Your Majesty's name to this country which was discovered by Friar Marcos of Nice, the provincial of the order of Holy Saint Francis. I described it all, and the sort of force I have, as Your Majesty had ordered me to relate in my letters; and stated that while I was engaged in the conquest and pacification of the natives of this province, some Indians who were natives of other provinces beyond these had told me that in their country there were much larger

---

[1] The text of this letter is printed in Pacheco y Cardenas, Documentos de Indias, vol. iii, p. 363, from a copy made by Muñoz, and also in the same collection, vol. xiii, p. 261, from a copy in the Archives of the Indies at Seville.

villages and better houses than those of the natives of this country, and that they had lords who ruled them, who were served with dishes of gold, and other very magnificent things; and although, as I wrote Your Majesty, I did not believe it before I had set eyes on it, because it was the report of Indians and given for the most part by means of signs, yet as the report appeared to me to be very fine and that it was important that it should be investigated for Your Majesty's service, I determined to go and see it with the men I have here. I started from this province on the 23d of last April, for the place where the Indians wanted to guide me.

After nine days' march I reached some plains, so vast that I did not find their limit anywhere that I went, although I traveled over them for more than 300 leagues. And I found such a quantity of cows in these, of the kind that I wrote Your Majesty about, which they have in this country, that it is impossible to number them, for while I was journeying through these plains, until I returned to where I first found them, there was not a day that I lost sight of them. And after seventeen days' march I came to a settlement of Indians who are called Querechos, who travel around with these cows, who do not plant, and who eat the raw flesh and drink the blood of the cows they kill, and they tan the skins of the cows, with which all the people of this country dress themselves here. They have little field tents

made of the hides of the cows, tanned and
greased, very well made, in which they live
while they travel around near the cows,
moving with these. They have dogs which
they load, which carry their tents and poles
and belongings. These people have the best
figures of any that I have seen in the Indies.
They could not give me any account of the
country where the guides were taking me.
I traveled five days more as the guides
wished to lead me, until I reached some
plains, with no more landmarks than as if
we had been swallowed up in the sea, where
they strayed about, because there was not a
stone, nor a bit of rising ground, nor a tree,
nor a shrub, nor anything to go by. There
is much very fine pasture land, with good
grass. And while we were lost in these
plains, some horsemen who went off to hunt
cows fell in with some Indians who also
were out hunting, who are enemies of those
that I had seen in the last settlement, and
of another sort of people who are called
Teyas; they have their bodies and faces
all painted, are a large people like the others,
of a very good build; they eat the raw flesh
just like the Querechos, and live and travel
round with the cows in the same way as
these. I obtained from these an account of
the country where the guides were taking
me, which was not like what they had told
me, because these made out that the houses
there were not built of stones, with stories,
as my guides had described it, but of straw

and skins, and a small supply of corn
there.

This news troubled me greatly, to find
myself on these limitless plains, where I
was in great need of water, and often had to
drink it so poor that it was more mud than
water. Here the guides confessed to me
that they had not told the truth in regard to
the size of the houses, because these were of
straw, but that they had done so regarding
the large number of inhabitants and the
other things about their habits. The Teyas
disagreed with this, and on account of this
division between some of the Indians and
the others, and also because many of the
men I had with me had not eaten anything
except meat for some days, because we had
reached the end of the corn which we carried
from this province, and because they made
it out more than forty days' journey from
where I fell in with the Teyas to the country where the guides were taking me, although I appreciated the trouble and danger
there would be in the journey owing to the
lack of water and corn, it seemed to me best,
in order to see if there was anything there
of service to Your Majesty, to go forward
with only 30 horsemen until I should be
able to see the country, so as to give Your
Majesty a true account of what was to be
found in it. I sent all the rest of the force
I had with me to this province, with Don
Tristan de Arellano in command, because it
would have been impossible to prevent the

loss of many men, if all had gone on, owing
to the lack of water and because they also
had to kill bulls and cows on which to sustain themselves. And with only the 30
horsemen whom I took for my escort, I traveled forty-two days after I left the force,
living all this while solely on the flesh of
the bulls and cows which we killed, at the
cost of several of our horses which they
killed, because, as I wrote Your Majesty,
they are very brave and fierce animals; and
going many days without water, and cooking the food with cow dung, because there is
not any kind of wood in all these plains,
away from the gullies and rivers, which are
very few.

It was the Lord's pleasure that, after having journeyed across these deserts seventy-
seven days, I arrived at the province they
call Quivira, to which the guides were conducting me, and where they had described to
me houses of stone, with many stories; and
not only are they not of stone, but of straw,
but the people in them are as barbarous as
all those whom I have seen and passed before this; they do not have cloaks, nor cotton of which to make these, but use the
skins of the cattle they kill, which they tan,
because they are settled among these on a
very large river. They eat the raw flesh like
the Querechos and Teyas; they are enemies
of one another, but are all of the same sort
of people, and these at Quivira have the advantage in the houses they build and in

planting corn. In this province of which the guides who brought me are natives, they received me peaceably, and although they told me when I set out for it that I could not succeed in seeing it all in two months, there are not more than 25 villages of straw houses there and in all the rest of the country that I saw and learned about, which gave their obedience to Your Majesty and placed themselves under your royal overlordship.

The people here are large. I had several Indians measured, and found that they were 10 palms in height; the women are well proportioned and their features are more like Moorish women than Indians. The natives here gave me a piece of copper which a chief Indian wore hung around his neck; I sent it to the viceroy of New Spain, because I have not seen any other metal in these parts except this and some little copper bells which I sent him, and a bit of metal which looks like gold. I do not know where this came from, although I believe that the Indians who gave it to me obtained it from those whom I brought here in my service, because I can not find any other origin for it nor where it came from. The diversity of languages which exists in this country and my not having anyone who understood them, because they speak their own language in each village, has hindered me, because I have been forced to send captains and men in many directions to find out whether there was anything in this country which could be of service to Your Majesty. And although I have searched with all diligence I have not found or heard of anything, unless it be these provinces, which are a very small affair.

The province of Quivira is 950 leagues from Mexico. Where I reached it, it is in the fortieth degree. The country itself is the best I have ever seen for producing all the products of Spain, for besides the land itself being very fat and black and being very well watered by the rivulets and springs and rivers, I found prunes like those of Spain [*or* I found everything they have in Spain] and nuts and very good sweet grapes and mulberries. I have treated the natives of this province, and all the others whom I found wherever I went, as well as was possible, agreeably to what Your Majesty had commanded, and they have received no harm in any way from me or from those who went in my company.[1] I remained twenty-five days in this province of Quivira, so as to see and explore the country and also to find out whether there was anything beyond which could be of service to Your Majesty, because the guides who had brought me had given me an account of other provinces beyond this. And what I am sure of is that there is not any gold nor any other metal in all that country, and the other things of which they had told me are nothing but little villages, and in many of these they do not plant any-

[1] Coronado had apparently forgotten the atrocities committed by the Spaniards at Tiguex.

thing and do not have any houses except of skins and sticks, and they wander around with the cows; so that the account they gave me was false, because they wanted to persuade me to go there with the whole force, believing that as the way was through such uninhabited deserts, and from the lack of water, they would get us where we and our horses would die of hunger. And the guides confessed this, and said they had done it by the advice and orders of the natives of these provinces. At this, after having heard the account of what was beyond, which I have given above, I returned to these provinces to provide for the force I had sent back here and to give Your Majesty an account of what this country amounts to, because I wrote Your Majesty that I would do so when I went there.

I have done all that I possibly could to serve Your Majesty and to discover a country where God Our Lord might be served and the royal patrimony of Your Majesty increased, as your loyal servant and vassal. For since I reached the province of Cibola, to which the viceroy of New Spain sent me in the name of Your Majesty, seeing that there were none of the things there of which Friar Marcos had told, I have managed to explore this country for 200 leagues and more around Cibola, and the best place I have found is this river of Tiguex where I am now, and the settlements here. It would not be possible to establish a settlement

here, for besides being 400 leagues from the
North sea and more than 200 from the
South sea, with which it is impossible to
have any sort of communication, the country is so cold, as I have written to Your
Majesty, that apparently the winter could
not possibly be spent here, because there is
no wood, nor cloth with which to protect the
men, except the skins which the natives
wear and some small amount of cotton cloaks.
I send the viceroy of New Spain an account
of everything I have seen in the countries
where I have been, and as Don Garcia Lopez
de Cardenas is going to kiss Your Majesty's
hands, who has done much and has served
Your Majesty very well on this expedition,
and he will give Your Majesty an account
of everything here, as one who has seen it
himself, I give way to him. And may Our
Lord protect the Holy Imperial Catholic
person of Your Majesty, with increase of
greater kingdoms and powers, as your loyal
servants and vassals desire.   From this
province of Tiguex, October 20, in the year
1541.   Your Majesty's humble servant and
vassal, who would kiss the royal feet and
hands:

FRANCISCO VAZQUEZ CORONADO.

TRANSLATION OF THE NARRATIVE OF JARAMILLO

ACCOUNT GIVEN BY CAPTAIN JUAN JARA-
MILLO OF THE JOURNEY WHICH HE MADE
TO THE NEW COUNTRY, ON WHICH
FRANCISCO VAZQUEZ CORONADO WAS THE
GENERAL.[1]

WE started from Mexico, going directly
to Compostela, the whole way populated and
at peace, the direction being west, and the
distance 112 leagues. From there we went
to Culiacan, perhaps about 80 leagues; the
road is well known and much used, because
there is a town inhabited by Spaniards in
the said valley of Culiacan, under the government of Compostela. The 70 horsemen
who went with the general went in a north-
westerly direction from this town. He left
his army here, because information had been
obtained that the way was uninhabited and
almost the whole of it without food. He
went with the said horsemen to explore the
route and prepare the way for those who
were to follow. He pursued this direction,
though with some twisting, until we crossed

[1] The text of this narrative is found in Bucking-
ham Smith's Florida, p. 154, from a copy made by
Muñoz, and in Pacheco y Cardenas, Documentos de
Indias, vol. xiv, p. 304, from the copy in the
Archives of the Indies.

a mountain chain, where they knew about New Spain, more than 300 leagues distant. To this pass we gave the name of Chichilte Calli, because we learned that this was what it was called, from some Indians whom we left behind.

Leaving the said valley of Culiacan, he crossed a river called Pateatlan (*or* Peteatlan), which was about four days distant. We found these Indians peaceful, and they gave us some few things to eat. From here we went to another river called Cinaloa, which was about three days from the other. From here the general ordered ten of us horsemen to make double marches, lightly equipped, until we reached the stream of the Cedars (arroyo de los Cedros), and from there we were to enter a break in the mountains on the right of the road and see what there was in and about this. If more time should be needed for this than we gained on him, he would wait for us at the said Cedros stream. This was done, and all that we saw there was a few poor Indians in some settled valleys like farms or estates, with sterile soil. It was about five more days from the river to this stream. From there we went to the river called Yaquemi, which took about three days. We proceeded along a dry stream, and after three days more of marching, although the dry stream lasted only for a league, we reached another stream where there were some settled Indians, who had straw huts and storehouses of corn and

223

beans and melons. Leaving here, we went
to the stream and village which is called
Hearts (Corazones), the name which was
given it by Dorantes and Cabeza de Vaca
and Castillo and the negro Estebanillo, because they gave them a present of the hearts
of animals and birds to eat.

About two days were spent in this village
of the Hearts. There is an irrigation stream,
and the country is warm. Their dwellings
are huts made of a frame of poles, almost
like an oven, only very much better, which
they cover with mats. They have corn and
beans and melons for food, which I believe
never fail them. They dress in deerskins.
This appeared to be a good place, and so
orders were given the Spaniards who were
behind to establish a village here, where they
lived until almost the failure of the expedition. There was a poison here, the effect of
which is, according to what was seen of it,
the worst that could possibly be found; and
from what we learned about it, it is the
sap of a small tree like the mastick tree, or
lentisk, and it grows in gravelly and sterile
land. We went on from here, passing through
a sort of gateway, to another valley very
near this stream, which opens off from this
same stream, which is called Señora. It is
also irrigated, and the Indians are like the
others and have the same sort of settlements
and food. This valley continues for 6 or 7
leagues, a little more or less.

At first these Indians were peaceful; and

afterward not, but instead they and those whom they were able to summon thither were our worst enemies. They have a poison with which they killed several Christians. There are mountains on both sides of them, which are not very fertile. From here we went along near this said stream, crossing it where it makes a bend, to another Indian settlement called Ispa.[1] It takes one day from the last of these others to this place. It is of the same sort as those we had passed. From here we went through deserted country for about four days to another river, which we heard called Nexpa, where some poor Indians came out to see the general, with presents of little value, with some stalks of roasted maguey and pitahayas. We went down this stream two days, and then left the stream, going toward the right to the foot of the mountain chain in two days' journey, where we heard news of what is called Chichiltic Calli. Crossing the mountains, we came to a deep and reedy river, where we found water and forage for the horses. From this river back at Nexpa, as I have said, it seems to me that the direction was nearly northeast. From here, I believe that we went in the same direction for three days to a river which we called Saint

[1] See Bandelier's Gilded Man, p. 175. This is Castañeda's " Guagarispa " as mistakenly interpreted by Ternaux-Compans, the present Arispe, or, in the Indian dialect, Huc-aritz-pa. The words "Ispa, que " are not in the Pacheco y Cardenas copy.

John (San Juan), because we reached it on his day. Leaving here, we went to another river, through a somewhat rough country, more toward the north, to a river which we called the Rafts (de las Balsas), because we had to cross on these, as it was rising. It seems to me that we spent two days between one river and the other, and I say this because it is so long since we went there that I may be wrong in some days, though not in the rest. From here we went to another river, which we called the Slough (de la Barranca). It is two short days from one to the other, and the direction almost northeast. From here we went to another river, which we called the Cold river (el rio Frio), on account of its water being so, in one day's journey, and from here we went by a pine mountain, where we found, almost at the top of it, a cool spring and streamlet, which was another day's march. In the neighborhood of this stream a Spaniard, who was called Espinosa, died, besides two other persons, on account of poisonous plants which they ate, owing to the great need in which they were.

From here we went to another river, which we called the Red river (Bermejo), two days' journey in the same direction, but less toward the northeast. Here we saw an Indian or two, who afterward appeared to belong to the first settlement of Cibola. From here we came in two days' journey to the said village, the first of Cibola. The houses have

flat roofs and walls of stone and mud, and
this was where they killed Steve (Estebanillo), the negro who had come with Dorantes
from Florida and returned with Friar Marcos de Niza. In this province of Cibola
there are five little villages besides this, all
with flat roofs and of stone and mud, as I
said. The country is cold, as is shown by
their houses and hothouses (estufas). They
have food enough for themselves, of corn and
beans and melons. These villages are about
a league or more apart from each other,
within a circuit of perhaps 6 leagues. The
country is somewhat sandy and not very
salty (*or* barren of vegetation [1]), and on the
mountains the trees are for the most part
evergreen. The clothing of the Indians is
of deerskins, very carefully tanned, and they
also prepare some tanned cowhides, with
which they cover themselves, which are like
shawls, and a great protection. They have
square cloaks of cotton, some larger than
others, about a yard and a half long. The
Indians wear them thrown over the shoulder
like a gipsy, and fastened with one end over
the other, with a girdle, also of cotton.
From this first village of Cibola, looking toward the northeast and a little less, on the
left hand, there is a province called Tucayan,
about five days off, which has seven flat-
roof villages, with a food supply as good as
or better than these, and an even larger

[1] Doubtless the reference is to the alkali soil and
vegetation.

population; and they also have the skins of cows and of deer, and cloaks of cotton, as I described.

All the waterways we found as far as this one at Cibola—and I do not know but what for a day or two beyond—the rivers and streams run into the South sea, and those from here on into the North sea.

From this first village of Cibola, as I have said, we went to another in the same province, which was about a short day's journey off, on the way to Tihuex. It is nine days, of such marches as we made, from this settlement of Cibola to the river of Tihuex. Halfway between, I do not know but it may be a day more or less, there is a village of earth and dressed stone, in a very strong position, which is called Tutahaco.[1] All these Indians, except the first in the first village of Cibola, received us well. At the river of Tihuex there are 15 villages within a distance of about 20 leagues, all with flat-roof houses of earth, instead of stone, after the fashion of mud walls. There are other villages besides these on other streams which flow into this, and three of these are, for Indians, well worth seeing, especially one that is called Chia,[2] and another Uraba,[3] and another Cicuique.[4] Uraba and Cicuique

---

[1] Acoma.　　　　　　　[2] Sia.
[3] Identical with Taos—the Braba of Castañeda and the Yuraba of the Relacion del Suceso.
[4] Pecos. In Pacheco y Cardenas this is spelled Tienique.

have many houses two stories high. All
the rest, and these also, have corn and beans
and melons, skins, and some long robes of
feathers which they braid, joining the feathers
with a sort of thread; and they also make
them of a sort of plain weaving with which
they make the cloaks with which they protect themselves. They all have hot rooms
underground, which, although not very clean,
are very warm.[1] They raise and have a very
little cotton, of which they make the cloaks
which I have spoken of above. This river
comes from the northwest and flows about
southeast, which shows that it certainly
flows into the North sea.

Leaving this settlement[2] and the said
river, we passed two other villages whose
names I do not know,[3] and in four days
came to Cicuique, which I have already mentioned. The direction of this is toward the
northeast. From there we came to another
river, which the Spaniards named after
Cicuique, in three days; if I remember
rightly, it seems to me that we went rather
toward the northeast to reach this river
where we crossed it, and after crossing this,
we turned more to the left hand, which
would be more to the northeast, and began

[1] All references to hot rooms or estufas are of
course to be construed to mean the kivas or ceremonial chambers.
[2] Tiguex is here doubtless referred to.
[3] One of the villages whose names Jaramillo did
not know was probably the Ximena (Galisteo) of
Castañeda.

to enter the plains where the cows are, although we did not find them for some four or five days, after which we began to come across bulls, of which there are great numbers, and after going on in the same direction and meeting the bulls for two or three days, we began to find ourselves in the midst of very great numbers of cows, yearlings and bulls all in together. We found Indians among these first cows, who were, on this account, called Querechos by those in the flat-roof houses. They do not live in houses, but have some sets of poles which they carry with them to make some huts at the places where they stop, which serve them for houses. They tie these poles together at the top and stick the bottoms into the ground, covering them with some cowskins which they carry around, and which, as I have said, serve them for houses. From what was learned of these Indians, all their human needs are supplied by these cows, for they are fed and clothed and shod from these. They are a people who wander around here and there, wherever seems to them best. We went on for eight or ten days in the same direction, along those streams which are among the cows.

The Indian who guided us from here was the one that had given us the news about Quevira and Arache (*or* Arahei) and about its being a very rich country with much gold and other things, and he and the other one were from that country I mentioned, to

which we were going, and we found these
two Indians in the flat-roof villages. It
seems that, as the said Indian wanted to go
to his own country, he proceeded to tell us
what we found was not true, and I do not
know whether it was on this account or because he was counseled to take us into other
regions by confusing us on the road, although
there are none in all this region except those
of the cows. We understood, however, that
he was leading us away from the route we
ought to follow and that he wanted to lead
us on to those plains where he had led us,
so that we would eat up the food, and both
ourselves and our horses would become weak
from the lack of this, because if we should
go either backward or forward in this condition we could not make any resistance to
whatever they might wish to do to us. From
the time when, as I said, we entered the
plains and from this settlement of Querechos, he led us off more to the east, until we
came to be in extreme need from the lack of
food, and as the other Indian, who was his
companion and also from his country, saw
that he was not taking us where we ought
to go, since we had always followed the
guidance of the Turk, for so he was called,
instead of his, he threw himself down in the
way, making a sign that although we cut off
his head he ought not to go that way, nor
was that our direction.

I believe we had been traveling twenty
days or more in this direction, at the end of

which we found another settlement of Indians of the same sort and way of living as
those behind, among whom there was an old
blind man with a beard, who gave us to
understand, by signs which he made, that
he had seen four others like us many days
before, whom he had seen near there and
rather more toward New Spain, and we so
understood him, and presumed that it was
Dorantes and Cabeza de Vaca and those
whom I have mentioned.

At this settlement the general, seeing our
difficulties, ordered the captains, and the
persons whose advice he was accustomed
to take, to assemble, so that we might dis-
cuss with him what was best for all. It
seemed to us that all the force should go
back to the region we had come from, in
search of food, so that they could regain
their strength, and that 30 picked horsemen
should go in search of what the Indian had
told about; and we decided to do this. We
all went forward one day to a stream which
was down in a ravine in the midst of good
meadows, to agree on who should go ahead
and how the rest should return. Here the
Indian Isopete, as we had called the companion of the said Turk, was asked to tell us
the truth, and to lead us to that country
which we had come in search of. He said
he would do it, and that it was not as the
Turk had said, because those were certainly
fine things which he had said and had given
us to understand at Tihuex, about gold and

how it was obtained, and the buildings, and
the style of them, and their trade, and many
other things told for the sake of prolixity,
which had led us to go in search of them,
with the advice of all who gave it and of
the priests. He asked us to leave him afterward in that country, because it was his native country, as a reward for guiding us, and
also, that the Turk might not go along with
him, because he would quarrel and try to
restrain him in everything that he wanted
to do for our advantage; and the general
promised him this, and said he would be
with one of the thirty, and he went in this
way. And when everything was ready for
us to set out and for the others to remain,
we pursued our way, the direction all the
time after this being toward the north, for
more than thirty days' march, although not
long marches, not having to go without
water on any one of them, and among cows
all the time, some days in larger numbers
than others, according to the water which
we came across, so that on Saint Peter and
Paul's day we reached a river which we
found to be there below Quibira.

When he reached the said river, the Indian recognized it and said that was it, and
that it was below the settlements. We
crossed it there and went up the other side
on the north, the direction turning toward
the northeast, and after marching three days
we found some Indians who were going
hunting, killing the cows to take the meat

to their village, which was about three or
four days still farther away from us. Here
where we found the Indians and they saw
us, they began to utter yells and appeared
to fly, and some even had their wives there
with them. The Indian Isopete began to
call them in his language, and so they came
to us without any signs of fear. When we
and these Indians had halted here, the general made an example of the Indian Turk,
whom we had brought along, keeping him
all the time out of sight among the rear
guard, and having arrived where the place
was prepared, it was done in such a way
that the other Indian, who was called Isopete, should not see it, so as to give him the
satisfaction he had asked. Some satisfaction was experienced here on seeing the good
appearance of the earth, and it is certainly
such among the cows, and from there on.
The general wrote a letter here to the governor of Harahey and Quibira, having understood that he was a Christian from the lost
army of Florida, because what the Indian
had said of their manner of government and
their general character had made us believe
this. So the Indians went to their houses,
which were at the distance mentioned, and
we also proceeded at our rate of marching
until we reached the settlements, which we
found along good river bottoms, although
without much water, and good streams which
flow into another, larger than the one I have
mentioned. There were, if I recall correctly,

234

six or seven settlements, at quite a distance from one another, among which we traveled for four or five days, since it was understood to be uninhabited between one stream and the other.

We reached what they said was the end of Quibira, to which they took us, saying that the things there were of great importance.[1] Here there was a river, with more water and more inhabitants than the others. Being asked if there was anything beyond, they said that there was nothing more of Quibira, but that there was Harahey, and that it was the same sort of a place, with settlements like these, and of about the same size. The general sent to summon the lord of those parts and the other Indians who they said resided in Harahey, and he came with about 200 men—all naked—with bows, and some sort of things on their heads, and their privy parts slightly covered. He was a big Indian, with a large body and limbs, and well proportioned. After he had heard the opinion of one and another about it, the general asked them what we ought to do, reminding us of how the army had been left and that the rest of us were there, so that it seemed to all of us that as it was already almost the opening of winter, for, if I remember rightly, it was after the middle of August, and because there was little to

---

[1] In Buckingham Smith's copy occurs the phrase, "que decian ellos para significarnoslo Teucarea." This is not in Pacheco y Cardenas.

winter there for, and we were but very little
prepared for it, and the uncertainty as to
the success of the army that had been left,
and because the winter might close the roads
with snow and rivers which we could not
cross, and also in order to see what had happened to the rest of the force left behind, it
seemed to us all that his grace ought to go
back in search of them, and when he had
found out for certain how they were, to winter there and return to that country at the
opening of spring, to conquer and cultivate it.

Since, as I said, this was the last point
which we reached, here the Turk saw that
he had lied to us, and one night he called
on all these people to attack us and kill us.
We learned of it, and put him under guard
and strangled him that night so that he
never waked up. With the plan mentioned,
we turned back it may have been two or
three days, where we provided ourselves
with picked fruit and dried corn for our return. The general raised a cross at this
place, at the foot of which he made some
letters with a chisel, which said that Francisco Vazquez de Coronado, general of that
army, had arrived here.

This country presents a very fine appearance, than which I have not seen a better in
all our Spain nor Italy nor a part of France,
nor, indeed, in the other countries where I
have traveled in His Majesty's service, for
it is not a very rough country, but is made
up of hillocks and plains, and very fine ap-

pearing rivers and streams, which certainly satisfied me and made me sure that it will be very fruitful in all sorts of products. Indeed, there is profit in the cattle ready to the hand, from the quantity of them, which is as great as one could imagine. We found a variety of Castilian prunes which are not all red, but some of them black and green; the tree and fruit is certainly like that of Castile, with a very excellent flavor. Among the cows we found flax, which springs up from the earth in clumps apart from one another, which are noticeable, as the cattle do not eat it, with their tops and blue flowers, and very perfect although small, resembling that of our own Spain (*or* and sumach like ours in Spain). There are grapes along some streams, of a fair flavor, not to be improved upon.

The houses which these Indians have were of straw, and most of them round, and the straw reached down to the ground like a wall, so that they did not have the symmetry or the style of these here; they have something like a chapel or sentry box outside and around these, with an entry, where the Indians appear seated or reclining. The Indian Isopete was left here where the cross was erected, and we took five or six of the Indians from these villages to lead and guide us to the flat-roof houses.[1] Thus they brought us back by the same road as far as

The pueblos of the Rio Grande.

where I said before that we came to a river
called Saint Peter and Paul's, and here we
left that by which we had come, and, taking
the right hand, they led us along by water-
ing places and among cows and by a good
road, although there are none either one way
or the other except those of the cows, as I
have said.   At last we came to where we
recognized the country, where I said we
found the first settlement, where the Turk
led us astray from the route we should have
followed.   Thus, leaving the rest aside, we
reached Tiguex, where we found the rest of
the army, and here the general fell while
running his horse, by which he received a
wound on his head which gave symptoms of
turning out badly, and he conceived the idea
of returning, which ten or twelve of us were
unable to prevent by dissuading him from it.

When this return had been ordered, the
Franciscan friars who were with us—one of
them a regular and the other a lay brother—
who were called, the regular one Friar Juan
de Padilla and the lay one Friar Luis de
Escalona, were told to get ready, although
they had permission from their provincial
so that they could remain.   Friar Luis wished
to remain in these flat-roof houses, saying
that he would raise crosses for those villagers with a chisel and adze they left him,
and would baptize several poor creatures who
could be led, on the point of death, so as to
send them to heaven, for which he did not
desire any other company than a little slave

238

of mine who was called Christopher, to be his consolation, and who he said would learn the language there quickly so as to help him; and he brought up so many things in favor of this that he could not be denied, and so nothing more has been heard from him. The knowledge that this friar would remain there was the reason that many Indians from hereabouts stayed there, and also two negroes, one of them mine, who was called Sebastian, and the other one of Melchor Perez, the son of the licentiate La Torre. This negro was married and had his wife and children. I also recall that several Indians remained behind in the Quivira region, besides a Tarascan belonging to my company, who was named Andrew. Friar Juan de Padilla preferred to return to Quivira, and persuaded them to give him those Indians whom I said we had brought as guides. They gave him these, and he also took a Portuguese and a free Spanish-speaking Indian, who was the interpreter, and who passed as a Franciscan friar, and a half-blood and two Indians from Capottan (or Capotean) or thereabouts, I believe. He had brought these up and took them in the habits of friars, and he took some sheep and mules and a horse and ornaments and other trifles. I do not know whether it was for the sake of these or for what reason, but it seems that they killed him, and those who did it were the lay servants, or these same Indians whom he took back from Tiguex, in return for the good deeds which he had done. When he was dead, the Portuguese whom I mentioned fled, and also one of the Indians that I said he took in the habits of friars, or both of them, I believe. I mention this because they came back to this country of New Spain by another way and a shorter route than the one of which I have told, and they came out in the valley of Panico.[1] I have given Gonzalo Solis de Meras and Isidoro de Solis an account of this, because it seemed to me important, according to what I say I have understood, that His Majesty ordered Your Lordship to find or discover a way so as to unite that land to this. It is perhaps also very likely that this Indian Sebastian, during the time he was in Quivira, learned about its territory and the country round about it, and also of the sea, and the road by which he came, and what there is to it, and how many days' journey before arriving there. So that I am sure that if Your Lordship acquires this Quivira on this account, I am certain that he can confidently bring many people from Spain to settle it according to the appearance and the character of the land.

[1] This is the spelling of Panuco in both texts.

TRANSLATION OF THE REPORT OF HERNANDO DE ALVARADO

ACCOUNT OF WHAT HERNANDO DE ALVA-RADO AND FRIAR JUAN DE PADILLA DISCOVERED GOING IN SEARCH OF THE SOUTH SEA.[1]

WE set out from Granada on Sunday, the day of the beheading of Saint John the Baptist, the 29th of August, in the year 1540, on the way to Coco.[2] After we had gone 2 leagues, we came to an ancient building like a fortress, and a league beyond this we found another, and yet another a little farther on, and beyond these we found an ancient city, very large, entirely destroyed, although a large part of the wall was standing, which was six times as tall as a man, the wall well made of good worked stone, with gates and gutters like a city in Castile. Half a league or more beyond this, we found another ruined city, the walls of which must have been very fine, built of very large granite blocks, as high as a man and from there up of very

[1] The text of this report is printed in Buckingham Smith's Florida, p. 65, from the Muñoz copy, and in Pacheco y Cardenas, Documentos de Indias, vol. iii, p. 511.

[2] Acuco or Acoma. The route taken by Alvarado was not the same as that followed by Coronado, who went by way of Matsaki. Alvarado's course was the old Acoma trail which led directly eastward from Hawikuh or Ojo Caliente.

good quarried stone. Here two roads separate, one to Chia and the other to Coco; we took this latter, and reached that place, which is one of the strongest places that we have seen, because the city is on a very high rock, with such a rough ascent that we repented having gone up to the place. The houses have three or four stories; the people are the same sort as those of the province of Cibola; they have plenty of food, of corn and beans and fowls like those of New Spain. From here we went to a very good lake or marsh, where there are trees like those of Castile, and from there we went to a river, which we named Our Lady (Nuestra Señora), because we reached it the evening before her day in the month of September.[1] We sent the cross by a guide to the villages in advance, and the next day people came from twelve villages, the chief men and the people in order, those of one village behind those of another, and they approached the tent to the sound of a pipe, and with an old man for spokesman. In this fashion they came into the tent and gave me the food and clothes and skins they had brought, and I gave them some trinkets, and with this they went off.

This river of Our Lady flows through a very wide open plain sowed with corn plants; there are several groves, and there

[1] Day of the nativity of the Blessed Virgin, September 8. This was the Tiguex or present Rio Grande.

are twelve villages. The houses are of
earth, two stories high; the people have a
good appearance, more like laborers than a
warlike race; they have a large food supply
of corn, beans, melons, and fowl in great
plenty; they clothe themselves with cotton
and the skins of cows and dresses of the
feathers of the fowls; they wear their hair
short. Those who have the most authority
among them are the old men; we regarded
them as witches, because they say that they
go up into the sky and other things of the
same sort. In this province there are seven
other villages, depopulated and destroyed by
those Indians who paint their eyes, of whom
the guides will tell Your Grace; they say
that these live in the same region as the
cows, and that they have corn and houses of
straw.

Here the people from the outlying provinces came to make peace with me, and as
Your Grace may see in this memorandum,
there are 80 villages there of the same sort
as I have described, and among them one
which is located on some streams; it is
divided into twenty divisions, which is
something remarkable; the houses have three
stories of mud walls and three others made
of small wooden boards, and on the outside
of the three stories with the mud wall they
have three balconies; it seemed to us that
there were nearly 15,000 persons in this village. The country is very cold; they do
not raise fowls nor cotton; they worship the

sun and water. We found mounds of dirt outside of the place, where they are buried.

In the places where crosses were raised, we saw them worship these. They made offerings to these of their powder and feathers, and some left the blankets they had on. They showed so much zeal that some climbed up on the others to grasp the arms of the cross, to place feathers and flowers there; and others bringing ladders, while some held them, went up to tie strings, so as to fasten the flowers and the feathers.

TESTIMONY CONCERNING THOSE WHO WENT ON THE EXPEDITION WITH FRANCISCO VAZQUEZ CORONADO [1]

AT Compostela, on February 21, 1540, Coronado presented a petition to the viceroy Mendoza, declaring that he had observed that certain persons who were not well disposed toward the expedition which was about to start for the newly discovered country had said that many of the inhabitants of the City of Mexico and of the other cities and towns of New Spain, and also of Compostela and other places in this province of New Galicia were going on the expedition at his request or because of inducements offered by him, as a result of which the City of Mexico and New Spain were left deserted, or almost so. Therefore, he asked the viceroy to order that information be obtained, in order that the truth might be known about the citizens of New Spain and of this province who were going to accompany him. He declared that there were very few of these, and that they were not going on account of any attraction

---

[1] Translated freely and abridged from the depositions as printed in Pacheco y Cardenas, Documentos de Indias, vol. xiv, p. 373. See note on page 377. The statements of the preceding witnesses are usually repeated, in effect, in the testimony of those who follow.

or inducement offered by him, but of their own free will, and as there were few of them, there would not be any lack of people in New Spain. And as Gonzalo de Salazar, the factor or royal agent, and Pero Almidez Cherino, the veedor or royal inspector of His Majesty for New Spain, and other citizens of Mexico who knew all the facts and had the necessary information, were present there, Coronado asked His Grace to provide and order that which would best serve His Majesty's interests and the welfare and security of New Spain.

The viceroy instructed the licenciate Maldonado, oidor of the royal audiencia,[1] to procure this information. To facilitate the hearing he provided that the said factor and veedor and the regidores, and others who were there, should attend the review of the army, which was to be held on the following day. Nine of the desired witnesses were also commanded by Maldonado to attend the review and observe those whom they knew in the army.

On February 26[2] the licentiate Maldonado took the oaths of the witnesses in proper form, and they testified to the following effect:

Hernand Perez de Bocanegra, a citizen of Mexico, stated that he had been present on the preceding Sunday, at the review of the

---

[1] Judge of the highest court of the province.
[2] Thursday.

force which the viceroy was sending for the pacification of the country recently discovered by the father provincial, Fray Marcos de Niza, and that he had taken note of the force as the men passed before him; and at his request he had also been allowed to see the list of names of those who were enrolled in the army; and he declared that in all the said force he did not recognize any other citizens of Mexico who were going except Domingo Martin, a married man, whom he had sometimes seen living in Mexico, and provided him with messengers; and one Alonso Sanchez, who was going with his wife and a son, and who was formerly a shoemaker; and a young man, son of the *bachiller* Alonso Perez, who had come only a few days before from Salamanca, and who had been sent to the war by his father on account of his restlessness; and two or three other workmen or tradespeople whom he had seen at work in Mexico, although he did not know whether they were citizens there; and on his oath he did not see in the whole army anyone else who was a citizen of Mexico, although for about fourteen years he had been a citizen and inhabitant of that city, unless it was the captain-general, Francisco Vazquez de Coronado, and Lopez de Samaniego the army-master; and, moreover, he declared that he felt certain that those above mentioned were going of their own free will, like all the rest.

Antonio Serrano de Cardona, one of the

magistrates of Mexico, who was present from beginning to end of the review of the preceding Sunday, testified in similar form. He said that Alonso Sanchez had formerly been a citizen of Mexico, but that for a long time his house had been empty and he had traveled as a trader, and that he was going in search of something to live on; and one Domingo Martin was also going, who formerly lived in Mexico, and whose residence he had not known likewise for a long time, nor did he think that he had one, because he had not seen him living in Mexico. He did not think it would have been possible for any citizens of Mexico to have been there whom he did not know, because he had lived in Mexico during the twenty years since he came to Mexico, and ever since the city was established by Christians, and besides, he had been a magistrate for fifteen years. And besides, all those whom he did see who were going, were the most contented of any men he had ever seen in this country starting off for conquests. After the force left the City of Mexico, he had been there, and had noticed that it was full of people and that there did not seem to be any scarcity on account of those who had started on this expedition.

Gonzalo de Salazar, His Majesty's factor for New Spain, and also a magistrate of the City of Mexico, declared that the only person on the expedition who possessed a repartimiento or estate in New Spain was

the captain-general, Vazquez de Coronado,
and that he had noticed one other citizen
who did not have a repartimiento. He had
not seen any other citizen of Mexico, nor of
New Spain, although one of the greatest
benefits that could have been done New
Spain would have been to draw off the young
and vicious people who were in that city
and all over New Spain.

Pedro Almidez Cherino, His Majesty's
veedor in New Spain, had, among other
things, noted the horses and arms of those
who were going, during the review. He
had noticed Coronado and Samaniego, and
Alonso Sanchez and his wife, whom he did
not know to be a citizen, and Domingo
Martin, who was away from Mexico during
most of the year. All the rest of the force
were people without settled residences, who
had recently come to the country in search
of a living. It seemed to him that it was a
very fortunate thing for Mexico that the
people who were going were about to do so
because they had been injuring the citizens
there. They had been for the most part vicious young gentlemen, who did not have
anything to do in the city nor in the country. They were all going of their own free
will, and were very ready to help pacify
the new country, and it seemed to him that
if the said country had not been discovered,
almost all of these people would have gone
back to Castile, or would have gone to Peru
or other places in search of a living.

Servan Bejarano, who had been in business among the inhabitants of Mexico ever since he came to that city, added the information that he knew Alonso Sanchez to be a provision dealer, buying at wholesale and selling at retail, and that he was in very great need, having nothing on which to live, and that he was going to that country in search of a living. He was also very sure that it was a great advantage to Mexico and to its citizens to have many of the unmarried men go away, because they had no occupation there and were bad characters, and were for the most part gentlemen and persons who did not hold any property, nor any repartimientos of Indians, without any income, and lazy, and who would have been obliged to go to Peru or some other region.

Cristobal de Oñate had been in the country about sixteen years, a trifle more or less, and was now His Majesty's veedor for New Galicia. He knew the citizens of Mexico, and also declared that not a citizen of Compostela was going on the expedition. Two citizens of Guadalajara were going, one of whom was married to an Indian, and the other was single. As for the many young gentlemen and the others who were going, who lived in Mexico and in other parts of New Spain, it seemed to him that their departure was a benefit rather than a disadvantage, because they were leading vicious lives and had nothing with which to support themselves.

When these statements and depositions had all been duly received, signed, and attested, and had been shown to his most illustrious lordship, the viceroy, he ordered an authorized copy to be taken, which was made by Joan de Leon, clerk of Their Majesties' court and of the royal audiencia of New Spain, the 27th of February, 1540, witnessed by the secretary, Antonio de Almaguer, and sent to His Majesty, to be laid before the lords of the council, that they might provide and order that which should be most serviceable to their interests.